101 MONEY SAVING MEALS

TRIED-AND-TESTED RECIPES

Hylas Publishing
Publisher: Sean Moore
Creative Director: Karen Prince
Designer: Gus Yoo
Editor: Beth Adelman

First Published in 2003 by *BBC Worldwide Ltd*,
Woodlands,

80 Wood Lane, London W12 0TT All photographs © BBC
Good Food Magazine 2003 and *BBC Vegetarian Good
Food Magazine* 2003

All the recipes contained in this book first appeared in
BBC Good Food Magazine and *BBC Vegetarian Good Food
Magazine.*

Published in the United States by
Hylas Publishing
129 Main Street, Irvington,
New York 10533

Copyright © BBC Worldwide 2002

The moral right of the author has been asserted.

Edited by Gilly Cubitt
Commissioning Editor: Vivien Bowler
Project Editors: Rebecca Hardie and Sarah Miles
Designers: Kathryn Gammon and Annette Peppis
Design Manager: Sarah Ponder
Production Controller: Christopher Tinker

First American Edition published in 2003
02 03 04 05 10 9 8 7 6 5 4 3 2 1

ISBN 1-59258-020-3

Set in Helvetica and ITC Officina Sans

Printed and bound in Italy by LEGO SpA

Color origination by Radstock Reproductions Ltd,
Midsomer Norton

Distributed by St. Martin's Press

101 MONEY SAVING MEALS
TRIED-AND-TESTED RECIPES

Editor-in-chief
Orlando Murrin

Contents

Introduction

As every cook knows, it's not how much money you spend on the ingredients that makes a great meal – it's what you do with them. So we've assembled our favorite low-cost recipes from *BBC Good Food Magazine* to prove that eating on a budget can be far from boring.

Forget franks and beans and baked potatoes with cheese, we've chosen a selection of stylish meals your family and friends will love that don't require special or luxury ingredients. Using the essentials you already have in your pantry and foods that are in season, we can help you conjure up something special every night of the week, like the *Apple Blackberry Ice Cream Sauce* pictured opposite (see page 192 for the recipe), without breaking the bank.

Our culinary teams have tried and tested each recipe to make sure they all work perfectly every time, and they've also kept the cost to a minimum without sacrificing flavor or quantities. Each recipe comes with a nutritional breakdown as well, so you can keep an eye on the calorie, fat and salt content.

This book guarantees you'll never again be short of quick, low-cost recipes for every season. It takes the stress out of weeknight suppers, and you'll be reminded that often the simplest things in life are the best.

Editor, *BBC Good Food Magazine*

Orlando Murrin

Conversion tables

NOTES ON THE RECIPES
• Eggs are large, unless stated otherwise.
• Wash all fresh produce before preparation.

OVEN TEMPERATURES

°F	°C	Gas	Fan °C	Oven temp.
225	110	¼	90	Very cool
250	120	½	100	Very cool
275	140	1	120	Cool or slow
300	150	2	130	Cool or slow
325	160	3	140	Warm
350	180	4	160	Moderate
375	190	5	170	Moderately hot
400	200	6	180	Fairly hot
425	220	7	200	Hot
450	230	8	210	Very hot
475	240	9	220	Very hot

APPROXIMATE WEIGHT CONVERSIONS
• All the recipes in this book use American measurements. The charts on this page and the next will help you convert to metric measurements. Conversions are approximate and have been rounded up or down. Follow one set of measurements only; do not mix the two.
• Cup measurements have not been listed here, because they vary from ingredient to ingredient. Please use a kitchen scale to weigh dry/solid ingredients.
• Where a recipe calls for a can of something (for example, tuna or tomatoes), we have listed what is generally a standard size can. If the standard cans in your area are a slightly different size, a small difference should not affect the outcome of the recipe.

SPOON MEASURES
• Spoon measurements are level unless otherwise specified.
• 1 teaspoon = 5ml
• 1 tablespoon = 15ml
• 1 Australian tablespoon = 20ml (cooks in Australia should measure 3 teaspoons where 1 tablespoon is specified in a recipe)

APPROXIMATE LIQUID CONVERSIONS

US	Metric	Imperial	Australia
¼ cup	50ml	2fl oz	¼ cup
½ cup	125ml	4fl oz	½ cup
¾ cup	175ml	6fl oz	¾ cup
1 cup	225ml	8fl oz	1 cup
1¼ cups	300ml	10fl oz/½ pint	½ pint
2 cups/1 pint	450ml	16fl oz	2 cups
2½ cups	600ml	20fl oz/1 pint	1 pint
1 quart	1 litre	35fl oz/1¾ pints	1¾ pints

A chunky and satisfying salad,
easily doubled for a crowd.

Tomato Salsa Salad

1lb 7oz tomatoes
4 scallions, chopped
2 tbsp chopped fresh parsley
1 garlic clove, finely chopped
4 tbsp olive oil
1 tbsp lemon juice
1lb 7oz new potatoes, halved
4 slices unsmoked bacon
4 hardboiled eggs
salt & pepper to taste
lettuce, to serve

Takes 30 minutes • Serves 4

1 Finely chop 8oz of the tomatoes and combine with the scallions, parsley, garlic, oil and lemon juice to make a salsa. Season to taste with salt and pepper. Cook the new potatoes in lightly salted boiling water until just tender. Drain and rinse under cold running water. Cut into thick slices.
2 Cook the bacon for 3–4 minutes over high heat until crisp. Allow to cool slightly then break into bite-sized pieces. Cut the remaining tomatoes and the eggs into eighths.
3 Toss the potatoes, eggs, tomato slices and salsa in a serving bowl. Season to taste. Scatter the bacon over the top and serve on a bed of lettuce.

• Per serving: 362 calories, protein 14g, carbohydrate 32g, fat 21g, saturated fat 4g, fiber 4g, added sugar none, salt 1.05g

Cubed feta cheese sold in jars of olive oil is ideal for this recipe.
Use the oil to make the dressing.

Warm Chickpea Salad

1 red onion, cut into wedges
2 zucchini, thickly sliced
1 red pepper, seeded and
cut into large chunks
13oz ripe tomatoes, halved
salt & pepper to taste
5 tbsp olive oil
juice of ½ a lemon
3 tbsp chopped fresh mixed herbs,
(chives, parsley and mint) or
3 tbsp chopped fresh parsley
2 × 15oz cans chickpeas, drained
4oz feta cheese, cut into cubes
pita bread, to serve

Takes 45 minutes • Serves 4

1 Preheat the oven to 425°F. Put the onion, zucchini, red pepper and tomatoes into a shallow roasting pan and season with black pepper. Drizzle with 2 tablespoons of the olive oil and toss well. Roast for 30 minutes, stirring halfway through, until the vegetables are tender.
2 Meanwhile, mix together the lemon juice and remaining olive oil and season with salt and pepper to taste. Stir in the herbs.
3 Allow the vegetables to cool for 5 minutes, then place them in a bowl with the chickpeas, feta and lemon and olive oil dressing. Toss lightly before serving with pita bread.

• Per serving: 375 calories, protein 15g, carbohydrate 29g, fat 23g, saturated fat 5g, fiber 8g, added sugar none, salt 1.62g

Double Gloucester cheese adds attractive color to the spinach.

Potato, Spinach and Cheese Melt

1lb 7oz new potatoes,
cut into long wedges
1 tbsp oil
8oz washed baby spinach leaves
4oz Double Gloucester
(or cheddar) cheese
salt & pepper to taste
1–2 tbsp snipped fresh chives
4oz thinly sliced smoked ham

Takes 25 minutes • Serves 4

1 Bring a large pot of salted water to a boil. Add the potatoes and boil for 12–15 minutes until tender.
2 Drain the potatoes well, then return to the pot. Add the oil and lightly toss the potatoes. Put the pot over a medium heat, add the spinach, cover and shake the pot occasionally until the spinach has wilted.
3 Cut the cheese into cubes or crumble it right into the pot. Season well with salt and pepper and add the chives. When the cheese starts to melt, spoon the salad onto warm serving plates. Using scissors, snip strips of ham over the top and serve immediately.

• Per serving: 289 calories, protein 16g, carbohydrate 27g, fat 14g, saturated fat 6g, fiber 3g, added sugar none, salt 1.31g

This salad looks most attractive when
you use Desirée or Romano potatoes.

Warm Potato and Broccoli Salad

1lb 9oz potatoes, cut into chunks
12oz broccoli, cut into florets
5 tbsp olive oil
1 onion, peeled and cut
into thin wedges
12 slices bacon
black pepper to taste
1 tbsp white wine vinegar
1 tbsp wholegrain mustard

Takes 40 minutes • Serves 4

1 Parboil the potatoes in salted boiling water for 5 minutes, adding the broccoli for the last 3 minutes. Drain the potatoes and broccoli.

2 Heat 2 tablespoons of oil in a pan. Add the onion and potatoes only, and cook for 8–10 minutes until golden. Meanwhile, cook the bacon until crisp, then drain on paper towels. Add the broccoli to the pan with the onion and potatoes and warm through. Put the vegetables in a bowl.

3 Add the remaining olive oil, vinegar and mustard to the pan the onion was cooked in, stirring until warm. Pour over the vegetables, toss gently and season with black pepper. Serve with the bacon on top.

• Per serving: 492 calories, protein 19g, carbohydrate 34g, fat 32g, saturated fat 9g, fiber 5g, added sugar none, salt 2.82g

A substantial main meal salad for all the family to enjoy. It's good served warm or cold.

Ham, Potato and Feta Salad

2lb 4oz new potatoes, halved if they are large
6oz feta cheese cubes in oil
1 tsp dried oregano
8 tomatoes, roughly chopped
4oz pitted black olives
salt & pepper to taste
8oz (about 4 slices) thick-sliced ham, cut into large pieces
handful of chopped fresh parsley

Takes 30 minutes • Serves 4

1 Bring a large pot of water to a boil (no need to add salt). Add the potatoes and cook for 15 minutes until tender.

2 Meanwhile, heat 2 tablespoons of the feta oil in a pan. Add the oregano and tomatoes and cook over a medium heat for 3–4 minutes, until slightly softened. Stir in the olives, feta cubes and ham, and stir well. Drain the potatoes and return to the pan.

3 Add the olive and tomato mixture to the pot with the potatoes and season with salt and pepper. Sprinkle on the parsley and toss lightly. Serve warm or cold.

• Per serving: 408 calories, protein 23g, carbohydrate 47g, fat 16g, saturated fat 7g, fiber 5g, added sugar none, salt 4.47g

Mix the ingredients, minus the avocado,
the night before serving for maximum flavor.

Salami, Bean and Avocado Salad

5oz pack white button mushrooms, sliced
8 radishes, sliced
½ small red onion, thinly sliced
15oz can cannellini, navy or great northern beans, drained
4 tbsp light olive oil
1 tbsp wine vinegar or cider vinegar
1 garlic clove, crushed
salt & pepper to taste
1 avocado
3oz peppered salami, sliced and each slice cut into eighths

Takes 15 minutes • Serves 4

1 In a bowl, toss the mushrooms, radishes, red onion and beans.
2 In a separate bowl, mix together the olive oil, vinegar and garlic. Season with salt and pepper.
3 Peel the avocado, remove the pit, and cut into chunks. Gently stir into the bean mixture with the salami and the dressing. Check the seasoning and serve immediately.

• Per serving: 362 calories, protein 11g, carbohydrate 14g, fat 29g, saturated fat 6g, fiber 6g, added sugar 2g, salt 1.24g

Grilled cheese for grown-ups,
but child's play to make.

Tomato Pizza Grilled Cheese

4 thick slices bread
4oz pesto sauce
8 tomatoes (about1lb 7oz),
thinly sliced
salt & pepper to taste
4oz cheddar cheese, grated

Takes 15 minutes • Serves 4

1 Preheat the broiler and toast the bread slices on one side. Turn over and spread a thin layer of pesto on the untoasted side.
2 Arrange the tomato slices over the top to cover. Season well with salt and pepper.
3 Sprinkle on the cheese and broil for 5 minutes, until the cheese is golden and bubbling. Serve immediately.

• Per serving: 380 calories, protein 17g, carbohydrate 25g, fat 24g, saturated fat 10g, fiber 2g, added sugar none, salt 1.36g

A quick and convenient pantry supper.
Be sure to use starchy potatoes to keep the mix together.

Tuna, Onion and Corn Hash

1lb 10oz starchy potatoes,
cut into chunks
bunch of scallions, chopped
6oz can tuna, packed in
water, drained
5oz frozen corn, defrosted, or
canned corn, drained
salt & pepper to taste
2 tbsp oil
2 large tomatoes, sliced
3oz cheddar cheese, grated
baked beans or salad, to serve

Takes 25 minutes • Serves 4

1 Cook the potatoes in salted boiling water for 12–15 minutes until tender. Drain the potatoes, return to the pot and mash thoroughly. Stir in the scallions, corn and tuna, and season well with salt and pepper.
2 Preheat the broiler to high. Heat the oil in a cast-iron frying pan. Add the potato mixture, spreading it out in the pan, and fry over medium heat for 4–5 minutes, until the bottom is brown and crisp.
3 Arrange slices of tomato over the potato and sprinkle with the grated cheese. Broil until the top is golden and bubbling. Cut into wedges and serve with baked beans or a salad.

• Per serving: 387 calories, protein 21g, carbohydrate 39g, fat 17g, saturated fat 6g, fiber 4g, added sugar none, salt 0.69g

Kids will love these and
they're great for barbecues, too.

BLT Burgers

1lb ground lamb, pork or turkey
salt & pepper to taste
2 tbsp Worcestershire sauce
4 slices smoked bacon
tomato slices, lettuce leaves,
mayonnaise and 4 burger buns,
to serve

Takes 30 minutes • Serves 4

1 Preheat the broiler to high, or light the
barbecue. Season the meat well with salt and pepper and stir in the Worcestershire sauce. Shape into
four burgers.
2 Cook the burgers under the broiler or on
the barbecue for 7–8 minutes on each side, until
completely cooked through. Cook the bacon alongside the burgers for the last 8 minutes of cooking
time, turning once, until crisp. Drain on paper
towels.
3 Fill the buns with sliced tomatoes and
lettuce leaves, then top with a burger. Lay
a slice of bacon on top and finish with
a spoonful of mayonnaise.

• Per serving: 433 calories, protein 32g, carbohydrate 27g, fat
23g, saturated fat 10g, fiber 1g, added sugar none, salt 1.76g

Chopped fresh apricots add juiciness and
a tangy flavor to ground pork.

Pork and Apricot Burgers

1lb ground pork
4 scallions, finely chopped
4 tbsp chopped fresh mint
2 firm, fresh apricots, about
6oz total, roughly chopped
1 egg, beaten
6oz plain, mild yogurt
salt & pepper to taste
4 burger buns and lettuce leaves,
to serve

Takes 30 minutes • Serves 4

1 Mix together the pork, scallions, 2 tablespoons of
the mint and the apricots. Season well and bind
together with the beaten egg. Divide the mixture
into 4 portions, and shape each portion into a burger.
2 Broil the burgers under moderate heat
or barbecue for 8–10 minutes on each
side. While the burgers are cooking, mix together the
yogurt and remaining mint, then season with salt
and pepper.
3 Serve each burger in a bun with some
lettuce, then spoon over the minty yogurt sauce.
Serve the rest of the sauce separately.

• Per serving: 300 calories, protein 30g, carbohydrate 5g, fat
18g, saturated fat 8g, fiber 1g, added sugar none, salt 0.35g

These kebabs make a lovely, lazy Sunday brunch. Prepare them the night before, then just broil them and cook the rice.

Bacon Kebabs on Mushroom Rice

2 medium leeks, each cut into 4 pieces
4 large, flat mushrooms (such as Portabello)
14 slices bacon, halved horizontally
4 herb sausages (such as sage sausage), halved vertically
10oz long grain rice
2oz butter, melted
1 tsp dried thyme
squeeze of lemon juice
6oz crème fraîche (or heavy cream mixed with 1/2 tsp buttermilk)
salt & pepper to taste

Takes 35 minutes • Serves 4

1 Blanch the leeks in boiling water for 3–4 minutes, then drain. Chop one mushroom and the stems of all the mushrooms, and set aside. Cut the other mushrooms into quarters. Assemble portions consisting of a piece of leek, a piece of mushroom and a piece of sausage. Stretch the bacon with the back of a knife, then wrap around each portion of leek, mushroom quarter and sausage. Thread onto skewers.

2 Preheat the broiler to high. Cook the rice. Melt half the butter with half the thyme and the lemon juice. Brush over the kebabs. Broil for 10 minutes, turning, until cooked.

3 Melt the remaining butter in a pan. Cook the reserved chopped mushrooms and remaining thyme until softened. Stir in the crème fraîche and season with salt and pepper. Stir the cooked rice into this sauce. Stir in the kebab pan juices. Serve immediately.

• Per serving: 1,023 calories, protein 27g, carbohydrate 73g, fat 71g, saturated fat 35g, fiber 1g, added sugar none, salt 4.72g

Mix the vegetables gently into the eggs so the dish doesn't break up too much.

Pea, Ham and Potato Omelette

1lb 7oz red potatoes, unpeeled
6 tbsp olive oil
1 onion, chopped
8 eggs
salt & pepper to taste
5oz thick-sliced ham, cubed
9oz frozen peas, thawed

Takes 45 minutes • Serves 4

1 Thickly slice the potatoes. In a large frying pan, heat 4 tablespoons of the oil. Saute the potatoes gently for about 15 minutes, until they are beginning to turn golden and just tender. Add the onion to the pan and cook for 5 minutes.

2 In a large bowl, beat the eggs and season well with salt and pepper. Add the potatoes, onion, ham and peas to the beaten eggs. Mix gently so you don't break up the potatoes.

3 Heat the remaining oil in the pan. Add the egg mixture and cook gently for 10 minutes until it is half set, then broil for 10–15 minutes until the top of the omelette is golden and just set. Cut into wedges and serve.

• Per serving: 516 calories, protein 27g, carbohydrate 36g, fat 30g, saturated fat 6g, fiber 6g, added sugar none, salt 1.33g

An Italian-style omelette made from ingredients
you're sure to have in your refrigerator.

Chunky Bacon and Cheese Frittata

8 slices thick slab bacon
bunch of scallions, sliced
8 eggs
2 tbsp milk
black pepper to taste
3oz cheddar cheese, cut into
small cubes
knob of butter
tomato salsa and thick slices of
bread, to serve

Takes 35 minutes • Serves 4

1 Shred the bacon into small pieces. Cook in a non-stick frying pan for 5–6 minutes until the fat begins to run. Drain off some of the fat. Add the scallions and cook for 5 minutes until it is tender and the bacon is crisp. Preheat the broiler to medium.

2 Beat the eggs and milk together and add pepper. Reserve a little bacon and mix the rest into the eggs with the scallions and cheese. Melt the butter in a 9-inch frying pan. Pour in the egg mixture and cook gently, without stirring, for 5–8 minutes until lightly set. Scatter the reserved bacon on top.

3 Slide the pan under the broiler to brown the top. Cut into wedges and serve with a chunky tomato salsa and bread.

• Per serving: 468 calories, protein 31g, carbohydrate 2g, fat 38g, saturated fat 16g, fiber 1g, added sugar none, salt 3.21g

You can bake the potatoes in the microwave for 20 minutes first,
but cook the eggs in the oven.

Baked Potatoes with Cracked Eggs

4 large baking potatoes
(about 1lb each)
1oz butter
5oz broccoli, cut into small florets
4oz mushrooms, sliced
salt & pepper to taste
8 eggs

Takes 1½ hours • Serves 4

1 Preheat the oven to 400°F. Bake the potatoes for
1–1¼ hours until they are cooked through and the
skins are crisp. About 5 minutes before the end of
the cooking time, melt the butter in a frying pan. Add
the broccoli and mushrooms and cook, stirring, for
about 3 minutes, then set aside.
2 When the potatoes are cooked, cut each in half
and scoop most of the flesh into a bowl. Stir in the
broccoli, mushrooms and pan juices. Season well
with salt and pepper. Spoon the mixture back into
the potato skins and use the back of a spoon to
make a small well in the middle of each. Set the
potatoes on a baking tray.
3 Carefully crack an egg into each well. (Don't worry
if the egg white spills over a little.) Return to the
oven and cook for 15 minutes until the eggs have
just set.

• Per serving: 358 calories, protein 19g, carbohydrate 35g, fat
17g, saturated fat 6g, fiber 4g, added sugar none, salt 0.52g

Choose large, starchy potatoes,
and serve for a light lunch or supper.

Cheesy Baked Potatoes

4 baking potatoes(about 12oz
each), scrubbed
salt & pepper to taste
2oz butter
4 tbsp milk
4oz cheddar cheese, grated
2 eggs, beaten
splash of Tabasco

Takes 1½ hours • Serves 4

1 Preheat the oven to 400°F. Rub the potatoes with a little salt, then transfer to a baking pan and cook for 1–1¼ hours, until tender. Remove from the oven and set aside until cool enough to handle.
2 Using a sharp knife, cut the tops off the potatoes and scoop the insides into a bowl, leaving the shells intact. Mash the potato flesh with a fork, beat in the butter, milk, 3oz of the cheese, the eggs and Tabasco. Season with salt and pepper. Spoon the mixture back into the potato shells.
3 Scatter the remaining cheese over the top and bake 20 minutes more, until fluffy and golden.

• Per serving: 509 calories, protein 18g, carbohydrate 61.1g, fat 23g, saturated fat 13.1g fiber 4.6g, added sugar none, salt 0.89g

Huge tomatoes make tasty containers for
a scrumptious stuffing.

Corn-Stuffed Tomatoes

4 large beefsteak tomatoes
pinch of sugar
salt & pepper to taste
2 tbsp olive oil
1 leek, thinly sliced
4 slices bacon, chopped
½ tbsp chopped fresh rosemary
3 slices day-old white bread
3oz frozen or canned corn
6oz gruyère cheese, diced
2 tbsp chopped fresh parsley

Takes 45 minutes • Serves 4

1 Preheat the oven to 400°F. Cut the tops off the tomatoes and discard. Using a spoon, scoop out the seeds to leave a hollow shell. Lightly season inside with a little sugar, salt and pepper, then put in a greased shallow baking dish.

2 Heat the oil in a frying pan and cook the leek, bacon and rosemary for 7 minutes, stirring occasionally. Meanwhile, cut the bread into cubes, then cook in the pan for 3 minutes, stirring to brown all over. Season, then add the corn, cheese and parsley.

3 Divide the stuffing between the tomatoes and bake for 20 minutes, until the filling is golden.

• Per serving: 321 calories, protein 15g, carbohydrate 22g, fat 20g, saturated fat 8g, fiber 3g, added sugar none, salt 1.46g

Cheesy, herby pastry puffs are good with
tomato sauce or with smoked fish.

Herbed Cheese Puff

2½oz all-purpose flour
pinch of mustard powder
salt & pepper to taste
2oz butter, cubed
4oz sharp cheddar cheese, grated
2 eggs, beaten
3 tbsp chopped fresh mixed herbs
steamed broccoli or leeks, to serve

FOR THE TOMATO SAUCE
1 tbsp olive oil
1 garlic clove, chopped or crushed
15oz can tomatoes
1 tbsp tomato paste

Takes 50 minutes • Serves 4

1 Preheat the oven to 425°F. Grease a baking sheet.
Sift the flour, mustard powder and a pinch of salt
onto a sheet of waxed paper. Bring the butter and ½
cup water to the boil. Stir in the flour, remove from
the heat and beat to a smooth, thick paste. Beat in
3oz of the cheese. Leave to cool for 5 minutes.
2 Gradually beat the eggs into the paste, one at a
time, then stir in the herbs. Drop spoonfuls on to the
baking sheet spaced slightly apart, to form an 8-inch
ring. Sprinkle over the remaining cheese.
3 Bake for 25–30 minutes until puffed up and crisp.
Meanwhile, put the tomato sauce ingredients in a
small pan. Season with salt and pepper. Bring to a
boil, stirring, then simmer for 10 minutes until thickened. Cut the puff into wedges. Serve with the sauce
and broccoli or leeks.

• Per serving: 340 calories, protein 13g, carbohydrate 18g, fat
25g, saturated fat 13g, fiber 2g, added sugar none, salt 0.88g

Choose a mild, soft cheese that doesn't overpower the flavor of the tomatoes.

Goat's Cheese and Tomato Tart

1 medium starchy potato, peeled
3oz cold butter, cut into pieces
1 onion, finely chopped
7 fresh thyme sprigs or 1 tsp dried
5oz all-purpose flour
salt & pepper to taste
1lb ripe tomatoes, thickly sliced
1 tbsp red wine vinegar
4oz soft goat's cheese
olive oil, for drizzling
salad, to serve

Takes 55 minutes • Serves 4

1 Preheat the oven to 400°F. Chop the potatoes, then cook in salted boiling water for 10–12 minutes. Drain and mash. Meanwhile, melt 1oz butter in a small pan and cook the onion until it is beginning to brown. Strip the leaves from 4 thyme sprigs and add to the pan, or add half the dried thyme.

2 In a bowl, rub the remaining butter into the flour. Add the onion, pan juices and mashed potatoes, and season with salt and pepper. Mix into a soft dough, then press into 9-inch round on a greased baking sheet.

3 Arrange the tomatoes on the dough and drizzle the vinegar on top. Sprinkle on the remaining thyme and season with salt and pepper. Crumble the cheese over and drizzle with oil. Bake for 35–40 minutes. Serve with a green salad.

• Per serving: 434 calories, protein 11g, carbohydrate 39g, fat 27g, saturated fat 16g, fiber 3g, added sugar none, salt 0.89g

Use your microwave to speed up
baking the potatoes.

Baked Potatoes with Leeks and Smoked Mackerel

4 large baking potatoes
2oz butter
2 large leeks (1lb 2oz),
thinly sliced
2 tbsp horseradish sauce
3 smoked mackerel fillets,
skinned and flaked
salt & pepper to taste
squeeze of fresh lemon juice

Takes 1 hour 10 minutes • Serves 4

1 Preheat the oven to 400°F. Bake the potatoes for about 1¼ hours, until crisp on the outside and tender all the way through.
2 When the potatoes are almost done, heat half the butter in a pan. Cook the leeks for about 6 minutes until softened, stirring regularly. Add the horseradish, sauce, flaked mackerel and lemon juice, and season with salt and pepper.
3 Halve the baked potatoes and fluff up the flesh with a fork. Pile the leek and fish mixture on top, dot with the remaining butter and serve hot.

• Per serving: 619 calories, protein 24g, carbohydrate 44g, fat 40g, saturated fat 13g, fiber 6g, added sugar none, salt 2.17g

Use frozen pizza dough or a premade crust
to keep preparation to a minimum.

Tuna Pizza Squares

frozen pizza crust, thawed, or
premade crust (about 10 inches)
2 tbsp olive oil, plus extra
for brushing
2 onions, thinly sliced
6oz can chopped tomatoes
½ tsp dried oregano
black pepper to taste
6oz can tuna, drained
3oz pitted black olives
2oz cheddar cheese, grated
green salad, to serve

Takes 35 minutes • Serves 4

1 Grease a 13 × 1-inch cookie sheet. Roll out thawed pizza dough on a floured surface to the same size as the pan. Put the dough in the pan and brush with olive oil. (Skip this step if you're using a premade crust.)
2 Preheat the oven to 400°F. Heat the oil in a frying pan and saute the onions until golden. Set aside. Spread the tomatoes onto the crust. Scatter the oregano on top and season with black pepper.
3 Break the tuna into chunks and arrange the tuna and olives on the crust. Scatter the onions and cheese on top and bake for 15–20 minutes, until the dough is risen, golden and cooked through. Cut into squares and serve with a salad.

• Per serving: 633 calories, protein 28g, carbohydrate 91g, fat 18g, saturated fat 5g, fiber 6g, added sugar 3g, salt 3.52g

Ready-made puff pastry and cheese sauce
make this quick to assemble.

Spinach and Ham Tart

9oz frozen leaf spinach
2 eggs
10oz your favorite cheese sauce
½ cup milk
black pepper to taste
8oz ham, thinly sliced
12oz sheet ready-made puff pastry
(thawed if frozen)

Takes 40 minutes • Serves 6

1 Preheat the oven to 400°F. Thaw the spinach in the microwave for 8 minutes on defrost. Pat really dry with paper towels. Beat the eggs into the cheese sauce, then add the milk and some freshly ground black pepper. Roughly tear each ham slice in half.
2 Unroll the pastry and roll it out a bit to line a 14 × 9-inch cookie sheet. Scatter the spinach over the pastry, then add the ham in rough folds. Pour the cheese sauce mixture over the tart.
3 Bake the tart for 25–30 minutes, until set and golden on top.

• Per serving: 414 calories, protein 18g, carbohydrate 30g, fat 26g, saturated fat 5g, fiber 1g, added sugar none, salt 2.21g

If you find anchovies a bit too salty,
rinse them in milk before adding them.

Pepperoni Pizza Tart

9oz ready-made pie crust
3 tbsp olive oil
1lb onions, thinly sliced
2 garlic cloves, crushed
2 x 15oz cans chopped tomatoes,
drained
1 tsp dried oregano
1oz thinly sliced pepperoni
3oz sharp cheddar cheese, grated
2oz anchovy fillets, packed in oil,
drained and halved lengthwise
12 black olives
salad, to serve

Takes 1¼ hours • Serves 6

1 Roll out the pie crust and line a 9-inch pie pan. Chill the crust while you make the filling.
2 Heat the oil in a pan and saute the onions and garlic for 15 minutes until soft. Cool for 10 minutes, then spread over the crust.
3 Preheat the oven to 425°F. Spread the tomatoes over the onions, sprinkle with oregano and top with the pepperoni. Sprinkle the cheese and arrange the anchovies and olives on top.
4 Bake for 25–30 minutes until the crust is cooked through. Serve hot or cold with a salad.

• Per serving: 376 calories, protein 10g, carbohydrate 28g, fat 25g, saturated fat 10g, fiber 4g, added sugar none, salt 1.68g

You can make one big cake by pressing
the mix into a frying pan instead. Grill the top.

Bubble and Squeak Cakes

1lb 9oz starchy potatoes,
cut into chunks
4 carrots, sliced
12oz green cabbage, shredded
2oz cheddar cheese, grated
6oz thick-sliced ham, cubed
bunch scallions, finely sliced
1–2 tbsp wholegrain mustard
1oz butter
2 tbsp oil

FOR THE SAUCE
15oz can chopped tomatoes
1 tbsp tomato paste
1 tsp sugar
salt & pepper to taste

Takes 40 minutes, plus chilling • Serves 4

1 Cook the potatoes and carrots in salted water for
15 minutes, until tender. Steam the cabbage for 8
minutes. Drain the potatoes and carrots well, return
to the pan and mash.
2 Stir in the cabbage, cheese, ham, half
the scallions and mustard to taste. Divide the mixture into 8 portions and shape into 4-inch cakes.
Chill for 30 minutes.
3 To make the sauce, cook the tomatoes,
the remaining scallions, tomato paste, sugar and salt
and pepper for 10 minutes.
4 Heat half the butter and oil in a frying pan. Fry 4
cakes at a time for 3–4 minutes on each side, until
golden. Keep them warm while frying the others in
the rest of the butter and oil. Serve with the sauce.

• Per serving: 423 calories, protein 21g, carbohydrate 45g, fat
19g, saturated fat 8g, fiber 9g, added sugar 1g, salt 2.03g

This contemporary variation on traditional fresh
pesto sauce is made from watercress, walnuts and lime.

Fettuccine with Watercress Pesto

12oz fettuccine
3oz watercress
4oz walnuts, chopped
2oz parmesan cheese, grated
1 garlic clove
finely grated zest and
juice of 2 limes
3½fl oz olive oil
salt & pepper to taste
Italian bread and tomato salad,
to serve

Takes 15 minutes • Serves 4

1 Cook the pasta in lightly salted boiling water
according to the package instructions.
2 Meanwhile, put the watercress, half the walnuts,
the parmesan cheese, garlic, lime zest and juice in a
food processor and process to a paste. With the
motor still running, gradually drizzle in the olive oil to
make a pesto. Season with salt and pepper.
3 Drain the pasta and return to the pot. Stir in the
pesto, then divide the pasta between serving bowls.
Scatter the remaining walnuts on top and serve with
Italian bread and a tomato salad.

• Per serving: 763 calories, protein 20g, carbohydrate 67g, fat
48g, saturated fat 8g, fiber 4g, added sugar none, salt 0.42g

Blue cheese can be substituted for brie, and
if you're not vegetarian, top with strips of crispy bacon.

Spaghetti with Tomato and Brie

10oz spaghetti
1lb 2oz zucchini, halved lengthwise
3 tbsp olive oil
2 garlic cloves, thinly sliced
finely grated zest and
juice of 1 lemon
6 ripe tomatoes, roughly chopped
5oz brie, diced
salt & pepper to taste

Takes 35 minutes • Serves 4

1 Cook the spaghetti in salted boiling water for
10–12 minutes until tender, or according to the
package instructions. Meanwhile, slice the zucchini.
Heat the oil in a large frying pan, then saute the
zucchini and garlic for 3–4 minutes until softened.
2 Add the lemon zest, tomatoes and
about 3 tablespoons of the pasta water (enough to
make a sauce). Cook a further 2–3 minutes until the
tomatoes begin to soften. Remove from the heat and
stir in the brie so it just starts to melt. Season with
salt and pepper and add lemon juice to taste.
3 Drain the spaghetti well and add to the tomato
sauce mixture. Toss well together, divide among
bowls and serve.

• Per serving: 490 calories, protein 19g, carbohydrate 62g, fat
20g, saturated fat 7g, fiber 5g, added sugar none, salt 0.66g

Roasting the vegetables makes them sweet, rich and satisfying.

Roasted Vegetable Pasta

2 zucchini, cut into sticks
1 red pepper, seeded and cut into strips
2 garlic cloves, finely sliced
3 tbsp olive oil
10oz pasta shells
6oz crème fraîche (or half-and-half mixed with 1/2 tsp buttermilk)
2 tsp wholegrain mustard
3oz cheddar cheese, grated

Takes 30 minutes • Serves 4

1 Preheat the oven to 425°F. Put the zucchini and red pepper in a roasting pan and sprinkle with the sliced garlic.
2 Drizzle with olive oil, then season and toss to make sure all the vegetables are coated with oil. Roast for 15–20 minutes, until the vegetables are tender and just beginning to brown.
3 Bring a large pot of salted water to boil. Add the pasta and cook for 10–12 minutes until just cooked. Drain, then stir into the roasted vegetables with the crème fraîche, mustard and grated cheddar. Serve immediately.

• Per serving: 490 calories, protein 19g, carbohydrate 62g, fat 20g, saturated fat 9g, fiber 4g, added sugar none, salt 0.58g

A quick supper made mostly from
ingredients you have in the kitchen cupboards.

Mushroom and Tuna Spaghetti

12oz spaghetti

FOR THE SAUCE
2 tbsp olive oil
1 garlic clove, chopped
6oz mushrooms, sliced
1 cup of frozen peas, thawed
6oz can tuna in water, drained
6oz crème fraîche (or half-and-half
mixed with 1/2 tsp buttermilk)
2 tbsp lemon juice
salt & pepper to taste

Takes 20 minutes • Serves 4

1 Cook the spaghetti in a large pot of salted boiling water for 10–12 minutes, until just tender.
2 Meanwhile, make the sauce. Heat the oil in a pan, then saute the garlic and mushrooms over a high heat for about 3 minutes, until the mushrooms start to soften. Add the peas and cook for another 2 minutes, stirring. Flake the tuna into the pan, then add the crème fraîche and lemon juice, and season with salt and pepper. Heat through gently.
3 Drain the pasta and return to the pot. Stir in the sauce and mix well. Serve on warmed plates with a fresh grind of pepper.

• Per serving: 516 calories, protein 26g, carbohydrate 73g, fat 16g, saturated fat 6g, fiber 6g, added sugar none, salt 0.72g

Look for smoked salmon ends and bits,
to keep costs down.

Tagliatelle with Smoked Salmon

1 tbsp vegetable oil
9oz button mushrooms, quartered
13oz dried or fresh tagliatelle
4–5oz smoked salmon, chopped
3 tbsp chopped fresh parsley
6oz crème fraîche (or half-and-half
mixed with 1/2 tsp buttermilk)
juice of ½ lemon
salad, to serve

Takes 20 minutes • Serves 4

1 Heat the oil in a frying pan. Add the mushrooms and cook for 8 minutes until they are beginning to brown.

2 Meanwhile, bring a large pot of salted water to a boil. Add the pasta and cook according to the package instructions.

3 Stir the salmon, parsley, crème fraîche and lemon juice into the mushrooms and season. Drain the pasta and quickly toss with the creamy sauce. Serve immediately with a salad.

• Per serving: 484 calories, protein 22g, carbohydrate 72g, fat 14g, saturated fat 6g, fiber 4g, added sugar none, salt 1.64g

Try adding pitted black olives or rinsed,
drained capers to this dish just before serving.

Tuna and Two Cheese Pasta

10oz penne
12oz broccoli florets
8oz cottage cheese with chives
5oz sharp cheddar cheese, grated
6oz can tuna in water, drained
salt & pepper to taste

Takes 20 minutes • Serves 4

1 Cook the pasta in a large pot of salted boiling water for 10–12 minutes until just tender, adding the broccoli florets to the pot for the last 3–4 minutes of cooking.

2 Drain the pasta and broccoli, then return to the hot pot. Gently stir in the cottage cheese and cheddar so it melts into the pasta.

3 Carefully mix in the chunks of tuna, trying not to break them up too much. Season with salt and pepper and serve.

• Per serving: 533 calories, protein 40g, carbohydrate 60g, fat 17g, saturated fat 9g, fiber 5g, added sugar none, salt 1.54g

Roast the tomatoes to emphasize
their sweetness and concentrate the flavor.

Tomato and Salmon Pasta

2 tbsp fresh oregano leaves,
or 1 tsp dried
2lb small ripe tomatoes
2 onions, sliced
1 garlic clove, finely chopped
2 tbsp olive oil
salt & pepper to taste
12oz spaghetti
1lb boneless, skinless salmon fillets
garlic bread, to serve

Takes 40 minutes • Serves 4

1 Preheat the oven to 400°F. If using fresh oregano, strip the leaves from the stems. Put half the oregano leaves, or all the dried oregano, into a roasting pan with the tomatoes, onions and garlic. Drizzle the oil on top. Season with salt and pepper, then stir well. Roast for 30 minutes, stirring occasionally, until the tomatoes have softened.

2 Cook the spaghetti in salted boiling water for 10–12 minutes, stirring occasionally. Meanwhile, cut the salmon into bite-size cubes. Add to the roasting pan for the last 5 minutes of cooking time.

3 Drain the pasta and spoon into the tomatoes and salmon. Sprinkle on the remaining fresh oregano, if using, and serve hot with garlic bread.

• Per serving: 615 calories, protein 36g, carbohydrate 77g, fat 20g, saturated fat 4g, fiber 6g, added sugar none, salt 0.19g

Store-bought stock (canned or bullion cubes) can be quite salty, so don't season this dish until the sauce is cooked.

Minted Chicken Rigatoni

12oz rigatoni
8oz fresh or frozen peas
knob of butter
1 tbsp vegetable oil
1 red pepper, seeded and sliced
4 boneless, skinless chicken breasts, cut into 1in cubes
1 onion, finely chopped
1 garlic clove, finely chopped
8fl oz chicken stock
4 tbsp chopped fresh mint, plus a few leaves as garnish
1 tbsp wholegrain mustard
6oz crème fraîche (or half-and-half mixed with 1/2 tsp buttermilk)
salt & pepper to taste

Takes 35 minutes • Serves 4

1 Cook the pasta in salted boiling water for 10–12 minutes, adding the peas for the last 3 minutes.

2 Heat the butter and oil in a large frying pan. Add the red pepper and cook for 5 minutes until it is starting to brown. Transfer to a plate. Add the chicken and onion to the pan and cook over high heat for 8 minutes, until the chicken is browned. Stir in the garlic for the last minute.

3 Add the stock, bring to a boil, then cook for 3 minutes to reduce by half. Stir in the red pepper, mint, mustard and crème fraîche. Season with pepper, and add salt if necessary. Drain the pasta, stir into the chicken and serve.

• Per serving: 718 calories, protein 51g, carbohydrate 80g, fat 23.8g, saturated fat 11.8g fiber 6.3g, added sugar none, salt 0.72g

You can use this all-in-one method
of sauce-making in other recipes, too.

Chicken and Spinach Pasta

12oz tubular pasta, such as penne
6oz frozen spinach
1 tbsp oil
4 boneless, skinless chicken thighs,
cut into strips
1 garlic clove, finely chopped
1½ cups 2% milk
1oz all-purpose flour
1oz butter
5oz sharp cheddar cheese, grated
freshly grated nutmeg to taste
salt & pepper to taste

Takes 50 minutes • Serves 4

1 Cook the pasta in salted boiling water
for 10 minutes, adding the spinach for the last 3–4
minutes of cooking time. Drain well. Meanwhile, heat
the oil in a wok or large pan, add the chicken strips
and garlic and stir fry for 3–4 minutes, until the
meat is well browned and cooked through. Remove
from the pan and set aside.
2 Add the milk to the pan, sprinkle in the flour, then
add the butter and whisk over medium heat until the
sauce is thickened and smooth. Stir in about 3oz of
the cheese and season with salt, pepper and
nutmeg to taste.
3 Preheat the broiler. Mix the chicken into the sauce
with the pasta and spinach. Spoon into an ovenproof
dish, sprinkle with the remaining cheese and broil
until golden.

• Per serving: 705 calories, protein 44g, carbohydrate 78g, fat
27g, saturated fat 13g, fiber 4g, added sugar none, salt 1.11g

*Soft cheese with herbs and garlic makes
an almost instant pasta sauce.*

Herb Pasta with Peas and Bacon

12oz tubular pasta, such as penne
12oz frozen peas
1 large red pepper, seeded and
cut into chunks
8 slices thick bacon
5oz soft cheese with herbs
and garlic
1 cup milk
black pepper to taste

Takes 20 minutes • Serves 4

1 Cook the pasta according to the package instructions. About 5 minutes before the end of the cooking
time, add the frozen peas and red pepper. Bring
back to a boil and cook for 5 minutes.
2 Meanwhile, cook the bacon until crispy. Cut into
bite-sized pieces.
3 Put the soft cheese and milk into a
large saucepan. Warm through, stirring
continuously, until it is smooth and thickened. Drain
the pasta and vegetables, and toss with the cheese
sauce and bacon. Season with freshly ground black
pepper.

• Per serving: 686 calories, protein 26g, carbohydrate 81g, fat
31g, saturated fat 16g, fiber 8g, added sugar none, salt 1.71g

A cheap and easy supper made from
readily available ingredients.

Leek, Pea and Ham Pasta

10oz spaghetti
6oz frozen peas
1oz butter
1 large leek
4 eggs
salt & pepper to taste
5oz thick-sliced smoked
ham, cut into cubes
3oz cheddar or Lancashire
cheese, grated

Takes 15 minutes • Serves 4

1 Bring a large pot of salted water to a boil. Add the
spaghetti and cook for about 10–12 minutes, adding
the peas for the last 3 minutes of cooking time.
2 Meanwhile, heat the butter in a small pan. Wash
and slice the leek. Add to the pan and cook over
medium heat for 3 minutes, until softened.
3 Beat the eggs in a bowl and season. Drain the
pasta and immediately return to the pot. Add the
leeks, eggs, ham and half the cheese. Stir well.
Adjust the seasoning, sprinkle with the remaining
cheese and serve.

• Per serving: 553 calories, protein 32g, carbohydrate 61g, fat
22g, saturated fat 10g, fiber 6g, added sugar none, salt 1.67g

Bacon, garlic and herbs, added to sage sausage,
give this sauce plenty of extra flavor.

Sausage and Tomato Spaghetti

1 tbsp olive oil
1 onion, chopped
1lb sage sausage
15oz can chopped tomatoes
1 bay leaf
pinch of sugar
salt & pepper to taste
12oz spaghetti
2 zucchini, cut into 2in sticks
2oz grated parmesan or
sharp cheddar cheese

Takes 45 minutes • Serves 4

1 Heat the oil in a pan, then saute the onion for 8 minutes, stirring occasionally, until golden. Remove the skins from the sausages and discard. Add the sausages to the pan and cook for 10 minutes, breaking them up with a spatula, until they start to brown .

2 Add the tomatoes, bay leaf and sugar, and season with salt and pepper. Bring to a boil, cover and simmer for 15 minutes until cooked.

3 Meanwhile, cook the spaghetti in salted boiling water for 10–12 minutes until tender, adding the zucchini for the last 5 minutes of cooking time. Drain, then stir into the sausage sauce with half the cheese. Serve hot with the remaining cheese sprinkled on top.

• Per serving: 690 calories, protein 33g, carbohydrate 78g, fat 30g, saturated fat 11g, fiber 4g, added sugar 1g, salt 2.92g

Red pesto is made from sundried tomatoes, basil, garlic, olive oil, Romano cheese and pine nuts.

Spicy Sausage Pasta

2 tbsp olive oil
6 good-quality sausages
1 onion, finely chopped
1 garlic clove, chopped
15oz can chopped tomatoes
1 tsp dried oregano
salt & pepper to taste
12oz penne or rigatoni pasta
1 tbsp red pesto

Takes 35 minutes • Serves 4

1 Heat the oil in a frying pan and cook the sausages over high heat for about 8 minutes until brown. Remove from the pan and cut into 1-inch pieces.

2 Saute the onion and garlic in the frying pan for 5 minutes. Add the tomatoes, sausage pieces and oregano, and season to taste with salt and pepper. Cover, reduce the heat and simmer for 10 minutes. Meanwhile, cook the pasta in salted boiling water for 10–12 minutes until just tender.

3 When the sauce has thickened, stir in the red pesto. Drain the pasta and return to the pot. Stir in the sauce and serve immediately.

• Per serving: 652 calories, protein 27g, carbohydrate 77g, fat 29g, saturated fat 8g, fiber 4g, added sugar none, salt 2.17g

Make double the amount of meatballs
and sauce, and freeze half for later.

Spicy Spaghetti with Meatballs

3 tbsp mixed fresh Mediterranean
herbs (basil, oregano, parsley
etc.), leaves stripped from their
stalks and minced
½lb ground pork
1 egg, beaten
1oz fresh breadcrumbs
2 garlic cloves, crushed
2 large onions, finely chopped
salt & pepper to taste
2 tbsp oil
2 tbsp tomato paste
2lb 4oz ripe tomatoes, chopped
½ tsp sugar
1 tbsp Dijon mustard
12oz spaghetti

Takes 1 hour 10 minutes • Serves 4

1 Mix the herbs with the pork, egg, breadcrumbs,
garlic and half the chopped onion, then season with
salt and pepper. Shape into 20 balls. Heat the oil in
a large frying pan. Saute the meatballs for 4–5 minutes, turning frequently, until browned, then remove
from the pan.
2 Saute the remaining onion until golden. Add the
tomato paste, tomatoes, sugar, 1½ cups water and
half the oregano. Simmer for 5 minutes. Process in a
food processor until smooth. Return to the pan.
3 Add the mustard and meatballs. Simmer for 25
minutes, then season with salt and pepper.
Meanwhile, cook and drain the spaghetti. Divide
among serving bowls and add the meatballs and
sauce. Sprinkle with the remaining oregano. Serve
immediately.

• Per serving: 689 calories, protein 41g, carbohydrate 88g, fat
22g, saturated fat 6g, fiber 7g, added sugar 1g, salt 0.77g

Quick-cook noodles with a peanut dressing
are topped with tender pork cutlets.

Peanut Noodles with Pork

8oz medium egg noodles
2 tbsp olive oil, plus extra
for cooing
4 pork cutlets, pounded thin
2oz salted peanuts
2 tbsp dark soy sauce
1 garlic clove, finely chopped
bunch scallions, sliced
4oz bean sprouts
black pepper to taste

Takes 25 minutes • Serves 4

1 Boil the noodles according to the package instructions. Meanwhile, heat a griddle pan and brush with a little oil. Season the pork cutlets, then saute for 2–3 minutes on each side until cooked through. Keep hot.
2 Put the peanuts in a plastic food bag and crush roughly with a rolling pin. Drain the noodles.
3 Mix together the olive oil, soy sauce and garlic, then toss with the noodles, scallions, bean sprouts and peanuts, and season with black pepper. Divide the noodles among four plates and top with the pork.

• Per serving: 581 calories, protein 45g, carbohydrate 49g, fat 24g, saturated fat 4g, fiber 2g, added sugar none, salt 2.02g

Make the most of quick-cooking ingredients to create an appetizing stir fry. For vegetarians, replace the pork with mushrooms.

Pork and Ginger Noodles

2 tbsp sunflower oil
1lb boneless pork, cut into thin strips about ½in wide
1in piece fresh ginger root, grated
2 garlic cloves, finely chopped
½ savoy cabbage, about 9oz, shredded
1 cup vegetable or chicken stock
1 tbsp soy sauce
4oz frozen peas
2 packets ramen noodles, cooked (without the seasoning) and drained
2 tbsp chopped fresh coriander, to serve

Takes 25 minutes • Serves 4

1 Heat the oil in a wok over a high heat, add the pork and stir fry for 3–4 minutes until just cooked. Stir in the ginger and garlic and continue to cook for 1–2 minutes.
2 Add the cabbage and stir fry with the pork until well combined. Pour in the stock and soy sauce.
3 Add the peas and noodles, stir well, then simmer for 5 minutes, until the cabbage is cooked but still crunchy. Scatter with coriander and serve.

• Per serving: 337 calories, protein 31g, carbohydrate 28g, fat 12g, saturated fat 2g, fiber 4g, added sugar none, salt 1.84g

Make extra marinade and keep it chilled,
ready to add a kick to your cooking.

Piri Piri Chicken

2 red chilies
1 red pepper
3 tbsp red wine vinegar
4 tbsp olive oil
salt & pepper to taste
4 boneless chicken breasts (skin on)
lettuce, to serve

Takes 30 minutes, plus marinating • Serves 4
(easily doubled)

1 Halve and seed the chilies and red pepper. Chop
the chilies finely and the pepper roughly. Place in a
food processor, add the vinegar and oil, and season
with salt and pepper. Process in a few pulses, but
leave chunky.
2 Slash the chicken breasts across the skin side
and put in a shallow ovenproof dish. Pour over
three-quarters of the marinade, turning the chicken
to coat it. Marinate for at least 10 minutes, or
overnight in the refrigerator if you have time.
Reserve the remaining marinade.
3 Heat a griddle or heavy frying pan, add the chick-
en and cook for 5–6 minutes each side, turning
once. Serve on a bed of lettuce with the reserved
marinade drizzled over the top.

• Per serving: 393 calories, protein 27g, carbohydrate 3g, fat
30g, saturated fat 7g, fiber 1g, added sugar none, salt 0.26g

A complete meal, with tender
chicken and warm new potatoes.

Griddle Chicken Salad

1lb new potatoes, halved
4 boneless, skinless chicken breasts
salt & pepper to taste
5 tbsp olive oil
juice of 1 lemon
handful of fresh chives,
finely snipped
4 tbsp sour cream
1 head romaine lettuce, shredded
9oz cherry tomatoes, halved

Takes 50 minutes • Serves 4

1 Cook the potatoes in salted boiling water for
15–20 minutes until tender. Meanwhile, pound the
chicken between two sheets of plastic wrap with a
rolling pin or mallet, and then season with salt and
pepper. In a large bowl, mix together the olive oil,
lemon juice and chives. Brush a third of the dressing
on the chicken.
2 Heat a griddle or large frying pan. Cook the chick-
en for 6–8 minutes, turning halfway. (You may need
to do this in batches.) Whisk the sour cream into the
remaining dressing and season with salt and pepper.
3 Drain the potatoes and leave to cool slightly, then
toss with another third of the dressing. Dress the lettuce and tomatoes with half the remaining dressing.
Divide between plates with the potatoes. Top with
the chicken and drizzle the remaining dressing on
top.

• Per serving: 412 calories, protein 37g, carbohydrate 22g, fat
20g, saturated fat 5g, fiber 2g, added sugar none, salt 0.29g

Substitute the same amount of dry white wine or cider
for the chicken stock, if you like.

Chicken with Cannellini Beans

2 tbsp olive oil
4 boneless chicken breasts (skin on)
½ tsp paprika
1 small onion, finely chopped
4oz bacon, finely chopped
8oz can chopped tomatoes
15oz can cannellini beans, drained
½ cup chicken stock
squeeze of lemon juice
2 tbsp fresh parsley, chopped

Takes 35 minutes • Serves 4

1 Heat the oil in a large frying pan. Season the chicken and sprinkle with paprika. Fry, skin-side down, for 8–10 minutes until the skin is golden and crispy. Turn and cook 5–6 minutes more, until the chicken is cooked through. Remove the chicken and keep warm.

2 Add the onion and bacon to the pan and cook for 5 minutes, stirring until the onion is cooked and the bacon is crispy.

3 Add the tomatoes, beans and stock. Stir well, then return the chicken to the pan. Bring to a boil, then reduce the heat and simmer for 2–3 minutes. Season, then stir in a squeeze of lemon juice. Sprinkle the parsley on top. Serve straight from the pan.

• Per serving: 455 calories, protein 38g, carbohydrate 15g, fat 27g, saturated fat 7g, fiber 5g, added sugar 2g, salt 1.52g

You can't beat fresh tarragon, but frozen,
available in supermarkets, will do.

Chicken and Tarragon Dauphinoise

2lb starchy potatoes
1 tbsp oil
1oz butter
1 small onion, finely chopped
1lb boneless, skinless chicken
breasts, cut into ½in strips
1 tbsp chopped fresh tarragon
6oz crème fraîche (or heavy cream
mixed with 1/2 tsp buttermilk)
salt & pepper to taste
6oz gruyère cheese, grated
green salad, to serve

Takes 55 minutes • Serves 4
(easily doubled)

1 Preheat the oven to 400°F. Butter a shallow oven-proof dish. Slice the potatoes thinly and cook in salted boiling water for 10 minutes until just tender. Drain well.

2 Meanwhile, heat the oil and butter. Saute the onion for 5 minutes until softened. Add the chicken and cook over high heat until nicely browned. Lower the heat, stir in the tarragon and half the crème fraîche, then season well with salt and pepper.

3 Spread half the potatoes in the dish. Spoon in the chicken mixture and cover with the remaining potatoes. Dot spoonfuls of the remaining crème fraîche on top and sprinkle with gruyère. Bake for 20–25 minutes until crisp and golden. Serve with a green salad.

• Per serving: 700 calories, protein 46g, carbohydrate 42g, fat 40g, saturated fat 21g, fiber 3g, added sugar none, salt 1.2g

*Use ground turkey for a change, and add
red pesto for a taste of the Mediterranean.*

Mediterranean Shepherd's Pie

2 onions
2 carrots
1 celery stalk
1lb lean ground meat,
such as turkey
4oz bacon, chopped
2 tsp all-purpose flour
10oz can vegetable or
other stock
½ cup red wine
1lb 9oz potatoes, peeled
knob of butter
salt & pepper to taste
4 tbsp red pesto
1oz parmesan cheese, grated

Takes 1¼ hours • Serves 4

1 Preheat the oven to 400°F. Chop the onions, carrots and celery in a food processor. Cook the meat in a pan over a low heat, stirring, until the juices start to run. Add the vegetables and bacon and cook for 15 minutes until browned.

2 Sprinkle in the flour and cook for 1 minute, still stirring. Stir in the stock and wine and cook, covered, for 30 minutes, stirring occasionally.

3 Meanwhile, cut the potatoes into chunks and boil for 10 minutes. Drain well, and return to the pot. Stir in the butter. Season with salt and pepper.

4 Stir the red pesto into the meat, season and spoon into a shallow ovenproof dish. Spoon the potato pieces on top, sprinkle with cheese and bake for 30 minutes until golden. Serve immediately.

• Per serving: 518 calories, protein 42g, carbohydrate 40g, fat 19g, saturated fat 6g, fiber 4g, added sugar none, salt 2.25g

Cooking the onions slowly caramelizes them,
adding sweetness.

Chicken with Sweet Onions

1 tbsp olive oil
1oz butter
3 onions, thinly sliced
2 garlic cloves, finely chopped
2 tbsp all-purpose flour
salt & pepper to taste
8 skinless chicken thighs
1 cup unsweetened apple juice
1 tbsp tomato paste
mashed potatoes or rice, to serve

Takes 1 hour • Serves 4

1 Heat the oil and butter in a large frying pan. Add the onions and stir well. Reduce the heat and cook gently for about 15 minutes, until they are softened and dark golden. Add the garlic for the last 5 minutes of cooking time.

2 Transfer the onions and garlic to a plate. Season the flour with salt and pepper. Dust the chicken with the flour, shaking off any excess. Cook in the pan for 10 minutes, turning halfway through.

3 Pour the apple juice into the pan with the chicken, then add the tomato paste. Stir well, scraping the bottom of the pan. Return the onions to the pan, cover and cook for 20–25 minutes, until the chicken is cooked through and the sauce has thickened. Serve with mashed potatoes or rice.

• Per serving: 369 calories, protein 40g, carbohydrate 24g, fat 13g, saturated fat 6g, fiber 2g, added sugar none, salt 0.57g

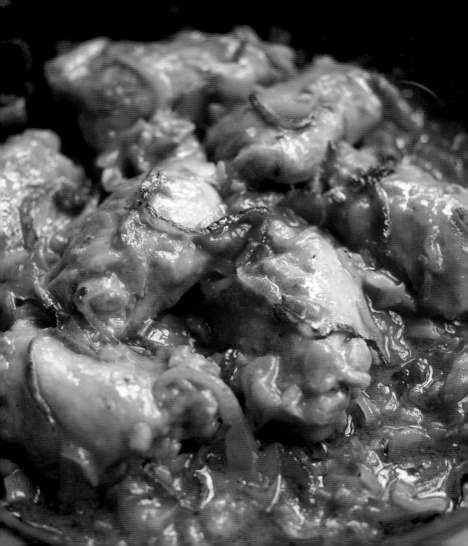

Invite everyone to assemble their own
tortillas at the table.

Chili Bean Tortillas

1lb ground beef, pork or lamb
1 onion, chopped
1 tsp mild chili powder
1 tsp ground cumin
15oz can chopped tomatoes
6oz can red kidney beans
salt & pepper to taste
8 flour tortillas
handful of shredded
iceberg lettuce leaves
grated cheddar cheese, sour cream
and lemon wedges, to serve

Takes 1 hour 10 minutes • Serves 4

1 Gently heat the meat in a frying pan to release some of the fat. Pour off. Increase the heat, add the onion and cook for 7 minutes, stirring occasionally to break up the meat. Add the chili powder and cumin and cook for 1 minute, stirring. Add the tomatoes and kidney beans and bring to a boil.

2 Reduce the heat, cover and cook for 30 minutes, until the meat is tender. Season with salt and pepper. Warm the tortillas in the microwave on High for 45 seconds, or wrap in foil and put in a preheated oven at 375°F for 5 minutes.

3 Top each tortilla with lettuce and spoon over some of the chili. Sprinkle with cheese and finish with a little sour cream and a squeeze of lemon juice, then fold the edges over to enclose the filling. Eat immediately.

• Per serving: 719 calories, protein 41g, carbohydrate 69g, fat 33g, saturated fat 18g, fiber 6g, added sugar none, salt 1.84g

Passata is made from chopped, strained tomatoes. If you can't find a version with added basil, you can add your own.

Baked Tomato Burgers

1 tbsp olive oil
1 large onion, finely chopped
1lb 2oz lean ground lamb or beef
3 tbsp chopped fresh basil
salt & pepper to taste
16oz jar passata with basil
(or strained puréed tomatoes)
green salad, to serve

Takes 50 minutes • Serves 4

1 Preheat the oven to 400°F. Heat the oil in a frying pan and cook the onion for about 5 minutes, until soft.

2 Put the meat and 2 tablespoons of the basil into a bowl, then add the softened onion and season well with alt and pepper. Mix until the ingredients are evenly combined. Shape into 8–10 flat burgers.

3 Pour about a quarter of the passata into a shallow baking dish. Put the burgers on top in a single layer. Heat the remaining passata and basil in the frying pan. Season with salt and pepper. Bring to a boil, then pour over the burgers. Bake uncovered for 30 minutes. Serve with a green salad.

• Per serving: 297 calories, protein 30g, carbohydrate 11g, fat 15g, saturated fat 6g, fiber 1g, added sugar 2g, salt 0.93g

There's a tendency to undercook new potatoes;
be sure they're tender before draining.

New Potato and Meat Curry

1lb lean ground beef or lamb
1 tbsp vegetable oil
1 small onion, chopped
3 garlic cloves, finely chopped
1 tbsp coarsely grated
fresh ginger
1 fresh red chili,
seeded and finely sliced
2 tsp ground cumin
2 tsp ground coriander
1 tbsp curry paste
1lb 2oz new potatoes
with skins, halved
salt to taste
4oz fresh spinach leaves, thickstems
removed, leaves torn if large
6oz plain, mild yogurt
chapatis or naan bread, to serve

Takes 1 hour • Serves 4

1 Heat a frying pan and add the meat. Brown it all over, stirring to break it up. Remove from the pan and set aside. Add the oil and onion to the pan and cook over medium heat for 5 minutes.
2 Stir in the garlic, spices and curry paste. Stir fry for 1 minute. Add the meat, potatoes and 2 cups water. Bring to a boil, cover, and simmer for 30 minutes. Season with salt to taste.
3 Stir in the spinach and simmer for 1 minute, uncovered, until wilted. Swirl in the yogurt and serve with Indian bread.

• Per serving: 353 calories, protein 32g, carbohydrate 26g, fat 14g, saturated fat 5g, fiber 2g, added sugar none, salt 0.54g

For a spicier taste, replace the bacon with 4oz
sliced chorizo or another spicy sausage.

Florentine Potato Gratin

2lb potatoes, any kind
6 thick slices bacon
12oz frozen spinach
(preferably individual leaves)
salt & pepper to taste
6oz crème fraîche (or heavy cream
mixed with 1/2 tsp buttermilk)
5oz gruyère or cheddar cheese,
coarsely grated

Takes 40 minutes • Serves 4

1 Preheat the oven to 400°F. Thickly slice the potatoes, then cook in salted boiling water for 7–10 minutes or until just tender. Drain. Meanwhile, cook the bacon until crisp and cut it into large pieces. If the spinach is frozen in a block, defrost it in the microwave. Otherwise heat gently in a pan. (Individually frozen leaves can be used straight from the freezer.)

2 Layer half the potato slices in a buttered shallow ovenproof dish (about 1 quart). Season lightly with salt and pepper, then spread the spinach on top and sprinkle with bacon. Top with the remaining potato slices. Season.

3 Dot with tablespoonfuls of crème fraîche, then sprinkle with the cheese. Bake for 25 minutes until golden and bubbling. Serve hot from the dish.

• Per serving: 617 calories, protein 26g, carbohydrate 41g, fat 40g, saturated fat 23g, fiber 5g, added sugar none, salt 2.49g

A colorful gratin that children will love.
Serve with boiled new potatoes or baked potatoes.

Leeks with Ham and Corn

4 leeks, trimmed and halved
widthwise, then washed
8oz thinly sliced ham
7oz can corn, drained
1 large tomato, seeded
and chopped
1oz butter
1oz all-purpose flour
1 cup milk
2 tsp wholegrain mustard
2oz cheddar cheese, grated

Takes 50 minutes • Serves 4

1 Preheat the oven to 400°F. Blanch the leeks for 2 minutes. Drain and refresh in cold water, then drain again really well.
2 Wrap each piece of leek in a slice of ham. Arrange them in a buttered 2-quart rectangular oven-proof dish. Scatter the corn and tomato over the top.
3 Put the butter, flour and milk in a pan and bring to a boil, whisking continuously until thickened. Stir in the mustard, simmer for 2–3 minutes, then pour over the leeks. Sprinkle with cheese and bake for 30 minutes until golden. Serve immediately.

• Per serving: 303 calories, protein 20g, carbohydrate 24g, fat 15g, saturated fat 8g, fiber 4g, added sugar 3g, salt 2.17g

Great for lunch boxes or picnics.
Vegetarians can replace the bacon with mushrooms.

Egg and Bacon Tart

9oz ready-made pie crust
5 eggs
4 thick slices bacon, chopped
1 large leek, chopped
1oz butter
1oz all-purpose flour
1 cup milk
2 tsp mustard
salt & pepper to taste
2oz cheddar cheese, grated

Takes 1¼ hours • Serves 4
(with leftovers)

1 Preheat the oven to 400°F. On a floured work surface, roll out the pie crust to an 11-inch circle. Line a 9-inch quiche pan or deep pie dish with the crust, and trim off any excess. Chill the crust for 15 minutes. Lightly prick the bottom with a fork, fill with crumpled foil and bake for 15 minutes.

2 Meanwhile, hard-boil two eggs for 8 minutes. Cool, then peel and chop. Fry the bacon and leek for 3 minutes until the bacon is crisp. Put the butter, flour and milk in a small pan. Bring slowly to a boil, whisking until thickened. Simmer for 2 minutes. Stir in the mustard.

3 Scatter the leek, bacon and chopped hardboiled egg over the crust. Beat the remaining eggs into the milk sauce, add the mustard and season with salt and pepper. Pour into the crust, add the cheese and bake for 40 minutes until puffed and golden.

• Per serving: 635 calories, protein 22g, carbohydrate 44g, fat 42g, saturated fat 23g, fiber 3g, added sugar none, salt 1.9g

Using ready-made pastry saves
preparation time.

Pea and Ham Tart

9oz ready-made pie crust
9oz frozen peas, thawed
4 eggs
6oz crème fraîche (or heavy cream
mixed with 1/2 tsp buttermilk)
3oz sharp cheddar, grated
3oz ham, cut into chunks

Takes 55 minutes • Serves 6

1 Preheat the oven to 400°F. Roll out the pie crust use it to line an 8–9-inch quiche pan or deep pie dish. Lightly prick the bottom with a fork, fill with crumpled foil and bake for 15 minutes.

2 Meanwhile, put the peas, eggs, crème fraîche and seasoning in a food processor and process until just blended. Stir in the cheese and ham.

3 Remove the foil from the pastry and lower the oven temperature to 350°F. Pour the filling into the pie crust. Bake for 35 minutes until the filling is golden and just set. Cool slightly before removing from the pan. Serve warm or cold.

• Per serving: 437 calories, protein 16g, carbohydrate 24g, fat 31g, saturated fat 16g, fiber 3g, added sugar none, salt 1.05g

Leftovers – if you have any –
make great packed lunches.

Ham and Pepper Tart

9oz ready-made pie crust
1 onion, finely chopped
1 garlic clove, crushed
1 red pepper, seeded and chopped
1 tbsp olive oil
8oz can chopped
tomatoes, drained
14oz thinly sliced ham
handful black olives (optional)
3 eggs
3 tbsp milk
salt & pepper to taste
salad, to serve

Takes 1 hour 10 minutes • Serves 4

1 Preheat the oven to 400°F. Roll out the pie crust
and use it to line a 9-inch quiche pan or deep pie
dish. Lightly prick the bottom with a fork, fill with
crumpled foil and bake for 15 minutes. Remove the
foil and bake another 5 minutes.

2 Saute the onion, garlic and red pepper in the oil
for 4 minutes until softened. Cool slightly. Lower the
oven temperature to 375°F. Pout the onion mixture
and tomatoes into the pie crust. Crumple the ham
between the vegetables. If using olives, scatter them
on top.

3 Beat together the eggs and milk, and season
with salt and pepper. Pour into the crust. Bake for
25–30 minutes until set. Serve hot or cold with a
salad.

• Per serving: 437 calories, protein 16g, carbohydrate 35g, fat
27g, saturated fat 10g, fiber 3g, added sugar none, salt 1.22g

A hearty dish that will appeal to the whole family.
You could substitute almost any type of beans.

Sausage and Bean Bake

2 tbsp olive oil
12 plump sausages
1 large onion, cut into wedges
6 thick slices bacon, chopped
4 celery stalks, sliced
2 garlic cloves, crushed
2 cups vegetable or
chicken stock
3 tbsp tomato paste
15oz can cannellini beans, drained
2 tbsp wholegrain mustard
salt & pepper to taste
garlic bread, to serve

Takes 40 minutes • Serves 6

1 Preheat the oven to 400°F. Heat half the oil in a frying pan, then brown the sausages all over. Transfer to a roasting pan.
2 Add the remaining oil, onion, bacon, celery and garlic to the frying pan, and saute until golden. Add the stock and tomato paste. Add the beans, scraping up any bits from the bottom of the pan. Let the stock bubble up, then pour into the roasting pan.
3 Bake, uncovered, for 15–20 minutes. Remove the pan from the oven and stir in the wholegrain mustard, then season with salt and pepper. Serve with hot garlic bread.

• Per serving: 429 calories, protein 23g, carbohydrate 18.2g, fat 30g, saturated fat 9.9g, fiber 3.5g, added sugar none, salt 3.41g

Soak wooden skewers in water for 30 minutes
before using, to prevent them from burning.

Pork, Apricot and Ginger Skewers

1 tsp oil
1 small onion, chopped
1 garlic clove, finely chopped
1lb ground pork or lamb
2in piece fresh ginger, grated
10 dried apricots, finely chopped
handful chopped fresh parsley
salt & pepper to taste
10oz long grain rice
½ tsp turmeric
juice of ½ lemon
5oz plain yogurt
rice, to serve

Takes 55 minutes • Serves 4

1 Preheat the oven to 400°F or the broiler to high.
Heat the oil in a pan, then saute the onion and garlic
for 5 minutes. Cool slightly, then put in a bowl with
the meat, ginger, apricots and half the parsley.
Season with salt and pepper.
2 Divide the mixture into four portions and mold
around the skewers. If cooking in the oven, transfer
to a roasting pan and cook for 20 minute.
Otherwise, place in a flat pan and broil, turning
occasionally, for 10 minutes until browned.
3 Boil the rice with 2 cups water and the turmeric,
covered, for about 12–15 minutes, until tender and
the water has been absorbed. Stir the rest of the
parsley and the lemon juice into the yogurt and
drizzle over the cooked skewers. Serve with rice.

• Per serving: 536 calories, protein 32g, carbohydrate 75g, fat
14g, saturated fat 5g, fiber 1g, added sugar none, salt 0.31g

Prepare the uncooked meatloaf, minus the topping,
the night before. Press into the pan, cover and chill.

Pork and Herb Meatloaf

1 tbsp oil
1 onion, finely chopped
2 thick slices bacon, chopped
1lb ground beef or pork
4oz fresh breadcrumbs
1 egg, beaten
1 tsp salt
2 tbsp tomato paste
1 tbsp dried tarragon or thyme
salad and new potatoes, to serve

FOR THE TOPPING
2 slices bacon
1oz breadcrumbs
2oz cheddar cheese, grated

Takes 1 hour 25 minutes • Serves 4

1 Preheat the oven to 350°F. Heat the oil in a frying pan and saute the onion for 3–4 minutes until softened. Transfer to a bowl. Mix in the bacon, beef or pork, breadcrumbs, egg, salt, tomato paste and dried herbs. Press into a 1-lb loaf pan. Bake, uncovered, 1 hour.

2 To make the topping, fry the bacon until crisp. Remove from the pan. Fry the breadcrumbs in the bacon fat for 2 minutes until just golden. Stir into a bowl with the cheese and crumble in the bacon.

3 Five minutes before the meatloaf is finished cooking, sprinkle the topping over the meatloaf. Return to the oven for 5 minutes to melt the cheese. Leave to stand for 10 minutes. Loosen the sides with a knife and remove. Slice and serve with a salad and new potatoes.

• Per serving: 488 calories, protein 37g, carbohydrate 29g, fat 26g, saturated fat 10g, fiber 1g, added sugar none, salt 3.01g

Roasting peppers brings out their sweetness. Canned roasted peppers may also be called pimentos.

Lemon and Thyme Meatballs

2 slices white bread, crusts removed, torn in pieces
2 tbsp milk
1 lb ground pork
finely grated zest of 1 lemon
2 tsp dried thyme
1 garlic clove, finely chopped
salt & pepper to taste
1 tbsp olive oil
1 small onion, finely chopped
9oz white mushrooms, sliced
10oz can roasted peppers, drained and chopped
6oz crème fraîche (or heavy cream mixed with 1/2 tsp buttermilk)
12oz rigatoni, cooked and drained, to serve

Takes 1 hour 10 minutes • Serves 4

1 Soak the bread in the milk for 5 minutes. Squeeze out the excess milk, then put the bread in a bowl with the meat, lemon zest, thyme and garlic. Season with salt and pepper. Mix well and shape into 20 balls.

2 Heat the oil in a frying pan. Cover and cook the meatballs for 20 minutes, turning, until they are evenly browned. Remove and keep warm.

3 Add the onion to the pan and cook for 5 minutes, until softened but not brown. Add the mushrooms and cook for 8 minutes until they are beginning to brown. Stir in the peppers and crème fraîche, heat through and season with salt and pepper. Stir the pasta into the sauce, spoon onto plates and top with the meatballs.

• Per serving: 753 calories, protein 38g, carbohydrate 73g, fat 36g, saturated fat 14g, fiber 4g, added sugar none, salt 0.67g

A simple topping makes ordinary pork
chops fit for a feast.

Pork Chops with Gorgonzola

4 large, boneless pork loin chops,
5–8oz each
1 tbsp olive oil
salt & pepper to taste
1 tbsp green pesto
3 small tomatoes, thinly sliced
4oz gorgonzola cheese,
cut into 4 thick slices
new potatoes and salad, to serve

Takes 20 minutes • Serves 4

1 Preheat the broiler. Brush the chops with the olive oil and season well with salt and pepper. Lay the chops on a baking sheet and broil for 4–5 minutes. Turn over and cook another 4–5 minutes.
2 Remove the chops from the broiler. Brush each one with the pesto. Put the tomato slices on top of the chops and add the slices of cheese.
3 Put the chops back under the broiler for 2–4 minutes, until the cheese is bubbling and has melted. Serve immediately with new potatoes and a salad.

• Per serving: 351 calories, protein 36g, carbohydrate 1g, fat 22g, saturated fat 9g, fiber none, added sugar none, salt 1.11g

This tasty relish keeps well in the refrigerator.
You can serve it with sausages or burgers, too.

Roast Pork with Onion Marmalade

2 x 10–12oz boneless pork chops
salt & pepper to taste
boiled potatoes, to serve

FOR THE MARMALADE
1lb onions, peeled and
thinly sliced
1oz butter
3oz light brown sugar
3½fl oz red wine vinegar

Takes 1 hour 5 minutes • Serves 4

1 Preheat the oven to 375°F. Put the pork chops in a roasting pan and season with salt and pepper. Roast for 25–30 minutes until cooked through.
2 Meanwhile, cook the onions in a pan with the butter for 10 minutes, until softened and lightly browned. Stir in the sugar and red wine vinegar and cook uncovered for 25–30 minutes more, stirring occasionally, until the onions are slightly caramelized and very soft.
3 Remove the pork from the oven. Cover with foil and leave for 5 minutes before slicing into thick pieces. Spoon the warm onion marmalade over the pork slices and serve with boiled potatoes.

• Per serving: 346 calories, protein 34g, carbohydrate 29g, fat 11g, saturated fat 5g, fiber 2g, added sugar 20g, salt 0.63g

Rösti are small cakes made of grated potato. Here, tuna is added
to make a meal of one frying-pan-size rösti.

Tuna Rösti

1lb 10oz potatoes, unpeeled
3 tbsp sunflower oil
1 large onion, sliced
6oz can tuna, drained
4 eggs
2 × 15oz cans baked beans

Takes 45 minutes • Serves 4

1 Cook the potatoes, in their skins, in salted boiling
water for 10 minutes. Meanwhile, heat a tablespoon
of the oil in a frying pan and saute the onion until
golden. Drain the potatoes and, when cool enough to
handle, peel. Grate them coarsely into a bowl. Add
the onion, tuna and seasoning and mix well.
2 Heat the remaining oil in the frying pan. Press the
potato mixture into it with a spatula to make a large
cake. Cook very gently for 10 minutes until the
bottom is golden.
Put a large plate on top of the pan and turn the rösti
out onto it. Slide it back into the pan and cook the
other side for 8–10 minutes.
3 Meanwhile, fry the eggs and heat up the beans in
a pan. Slide the rösti out of the pan onto a serving
plate. Cut into wedges and serve with the fried eggs
and baked beans.

• Per serving: 511 calories, protein 30g, carbohydrate 67g, fat
16g, saturated fat 3g, fiber 10g, added sugar 7g, salt 3.34g

Puff pastry rectangles,
cooked separately, become the pie lids.

Easy Tuna Puff Pie

12oz package ready-to-use
puff pastry
1oz butter
1 onion, chopped
1 small red pepper,
seeded and chopped
1oz all-purpose flour
2 cups milk
1lb 9oz potatoes, peeled and
cut into big chunks
8oz broccoli, cut into florets
6oz can chunk white tuna
in water, drained
salt & pepper to taste
handful chopped fresh parsley

Takes 45 minutes • Serves 4

1 Preheat the oven to 400°F. Spread out the puff pastry and cut out four 5 × 4-inch rectangles. Place on a baking sheet, lightly score the tops diagonally and bake for 15–18 minutes, until they are golden and puffed.
2 Meanwhile, melt the butter in a pan, then saute the onion and pepper until soft but not brown. Add the flour and cook, stirring, 1 minute. Gradually stir in the milk. Cook, stirring, until it is slightly thickened.
3 Add the potatoes and simmer, covered, for 10 minutes. Add the broccoli and simmer for 10 more minutes until tender. Stir the tuna into the sauce and heat through. Season with salt and pepper, add the parsley and spoon on to serving plates. Top each serving with a pastry lid.

• Per serving: 721 calories, protein 26g, carbohydrate 82g, fat 34g, saturated fat 7g, fiber 5g, added sugar none, salt 1.42g

A bit of pesto makes an instant, tasty dressing.
The spinach softens in the heat of the potatoes.

Warm Potato and Tuna Salad

1lb 7oz new potatoes,
halved lengthwise if large
2 tbsp pesto (fresh is best)
4 tbsp olive oil
8 cherry tomatoes
6oz can tuna, drained
8oz green beans, halved
few handfuls spinach (preferably
baby leaves, tear if larger)
salt & pepper to taste
crusty bread, to serve

Takes 20 minutes • Serves 4

1 Put the potatoes in a pan of salted boiling water, bring back to a boil and simmer for 8–10 minutes.
2 Meanwhile, mix together the pesto and oil. Halve the tomatoes, and drain and flake the tuna. Add the beans to the potatoes for the last 3 minutes of cooking time.
3 Drain the potatoes and beans and put in a salad bowl. Stir in the spinach so it wilts a little in the warmth from the vegetables. Season with salt and pepper. Scatter the tomatoes and tuna, drizzle the pesto over everything and toss. Serve with crusty bread.

• Per serving: 336 calories, protein 15g, carbohydrate 28g, fat 19g, saturated fat 3g, fiber 3g, added sugar none, salt 0.45g

Instead of using canned soup, you could use mushroom or tomato sauce from a jar or the freezer.

Tuna and Broccoli Pasta Bake

10oz penne or rigatoni
14oz broccoli, cut into small florets
6oz can tuna, drained
10oz can condensed mushroom soup
½ cup milk
4oz cheddar cheese, grated
1 small package potato chips

Takes 30 minutes • Serves 4

1 Preheat the oven to 400°F. Cook the pasta in salted boiling water for 10–12 minutes. Add the broccoli for the last 3 minutes of cooking, then drain.

2 Put the pasta and broccoli into a shallow oven-proof dish. Scatter the tuna on top. Mix the soup with the milk, then pour over the pasta and gently toss.

3 Sprinkle on two-thirds of the cheese. Lightly crush the crisps in the bag, then sprinkle over the pasta. Top with the remaining cheese. Bake for 15 minutes until the topping is golden. Serve immediately.

• Per serving: 572 calories, protein 33g, carbohydrate 69g, fat 20g, saturated fat 8g, fiber 5g, added sugar none, salt 2.41g

A simple and filling supper made
from a can of salmon.

Potato and Salmon Grill

1lb 7oz new potatoes, skin on,
sliced lengthwise
4oz frozen peas
6oz can salmon
salt & pepper to taste
6oz crème fraîche (or heavy cream
mixed with 1/2 tsp buttermilk)
4oz sharp cheddar cheese,
coarsely grated

Takes 25 minutes • Serves 4

1 Boil the potatoes in salted water for about 10 minutes, until almost tender but not breaking up. Add the frozen peas and simmer for another 2–3 minutes. Drain well, then put in a mixing bowl. Preheat the broiler.

2 Drain the salmon and flake into chunks, then gently toss with the potatoes and peas. Season with salt and pepper and spoon into a shallow flameproof dish.

3 Dollop the crème fraîche on top, roughly spread it over the dish, then scatter the cheese. Grill for a few minutes until bubbling and golden.

• Per serving: 465 calories, protein 22g, carbohydrate 31g, fat 29g, saturated fat 15g, fiber 3g, added sugar none, salt 1.10g

Think you don't have time to make a casserole?
You do in a microwave.

Salmon and Corn Casserole

2 leeks, about 10oz total
1lb 9oz starchy potatoes
1 cup whole milk
1 cup vegetable stock
6oz can corn, drained
1lb skinless salmon fillets,
cut into 1in cubes
salt & pepper to taste
good splash of Tabasco
handful of chopped fresh parsley

Takes 25 minutes • Serves 4

1 Halve the leeks lengthwise, then slice. Set aside. Peel the potatoes, cut into cubes and put in a microwave-proof bowl with the milk and stock.
2 Microwave the potatoes on High for 8 minutes until they're starting to soften. Add the leeks and cook for 5 minutes. Stir well with a fork, pressing about half the potato cubes against the side of the bowl to break up and thicken the stock.
3 Stir in the corn and salmon, and season with salt and pepper. Microwave on High for 3 minutes until the salmon is just cooked through. Stir in the Tabasco and parsley. Serve immediately.

• Per serving: 453 calories, protein 32g, carbohydrate 47g, fat 17g, saturated fat 4g, fiber 5g, added sugar 3g, salt 0.85g

Salmon fillets are always on sale
somewhere, but still seem luxurious.

Orange Crumb Salmon

3oz fresh breadcrumbs (from
2 thick slices white bread)
2 tbsp olive oil, plus extra
for cooking
finely grated zest and
juice of 1 orange
4 tbsp chopped fresh parsley
salt & pepper to taste
4 skinless salmon fillets,
about 5oz each
1lb 9oz new potatoes
3 tbsp mayonnaise

Takes 35 minutes • Serves 4

1 Preheat the oven to 400°F. Mix together the breadcrumbs, oil, orange zest and half the parsley. Season with salt and pepper.

2 Put the salmon fillets on a baking sheet lined with lightly greased foil. Press the orange crumbs onto each fillet so they stick. Bake for 15–20 minutes until the salmon is just cooked and the topping is golden.

3 Meanwhile, cook the potatoes in a pot of salted boiling water for 12–15 minutes until tender, then drain. Stir the remaining parsley into the mayonnaise and thin with a little bit of the orange juice, until it has the consistency of cream. Serve the salmon with the new potatoes and the orange mayonnaise.

• Per serving: 611 calories, protein 34g, carbohydrate 46g, fat 33g, saturated fat 6g, fiber 3g, added sugar none, salt 0.8g

You could use well-drained canned
salmon instead of fresh fish.

Salmon and Dill Fishcakes

1lb 9oz potatoes, cut into chunks
3½fl oz milk
10oz skinless salmon fillets
knob of butter
1 small onion, finely chopped
2 tsp creamed horseradish sauce
1 heaped tbsp chopped fresh dill
salt & pepper to taste
vegetable oil, for frying
1 egg, beaten
8oz dry breadcrumbs
potato chips or new potatoes,
and tomato and onion salad,
to serve

Takes 40 minutes • Serves 4

1 Cook the potatoes in salted boiling water for 15 minutes until tender. Drain and mash. Put the milk and salmon in a frying pan. Bring just to a boil, cover with foil and simmer for 3–4 minutes until just cooked. remove from the heat and let stand for 5 minutes. Drain and flake the fish. Reserve the milk.

2 Heat the butter in a pan and cook the onion for 3–4 minutes. Mix into the potatoes with two table-spoons of the reserved milk, the horseradish sauce and dill. Season with salt and pepper. Stir in the flaked fish.

3 Divide the mixture into 8 portions and shape into cakes. Heat ½ inch oil in a frying pan. Dip each cake in egg, then breadcrumbs. Fry for 5 minutes, turning halfway, until golden. Serve with potato chips or boiled new potatoes and a salad.

• Per serving: 644 calories, protein 27g, carbohydrate 72g, fat 92g, saturated fat 6g, fiber 4g, added sugar none, salt 1.27g

Crushed crackers make an especially
crispy coating for fishcakes.

Crisp Cod and Corn Cakes

4 tbsp milk
1lb 2oz cod fillets
7oz can corn, drained
6 scallions, finely chopped
1lb 10oz starchy potatoes,
cooked and mashed with butter
salt & pepper to taste
2 eggs
12 crackers, crushed into
fine crumbs
oil, for shallow frying
salad and tomato salsa,
to serve

Takes 35 minutes • Serves 4

1 Put the milk and fish in a frying pan. Bring just to
a boil, cover and cook for 4–5 minutes, depending
on the thickness of the fish. It should flake easily.
Set aside until cool enough to handle.

2 Stir the corn and onions into the mashed potatoes
and season with salt and pepper. Remove the fish
with a slotted spoon and stir into the potatoes, tak-
ing care not to break up the fish too much. Divide
into 8 portions and shape into round cakes.

3 Beat the eggs lightly with a fork. Dip the cakes in
the egg, then in the cracker crumbs. Heat a little oil
in a frying pan and cook the cakes, 4 at a time, for
about 3 minutes. Carefully turn and cook for
2–3 minutes until crisp and golden. Serve with a
salad and some tomato salsa.

• Per serving: 628 calories, protein 33g, carbohydrate 57g, fat
31g, saturated fat 8g, fiber 3g, added sugar 3g, salt 1.3g

Eat mackerel when it is as fresh as possible and still glossy, for the best flavor.

Mackerel Baked in Foil

2 whole mackerel
salt & pepper to taste
1 lemon
4 fresh rosemary sprigs
2 garlic cloves, sliced
1 small red onion, thinly sliced
4 tbsp cider or apple juice
boiled potatoes, sprinkled with parsley, to serve

Takes 30 minutes • Serves 2

1 Preheat the oven to 400°F. Put each fish on a large square of foil on a baking sheet. Season the fish inside and out with salt and pepper.

2 Slice the lemon, then cut each slice in half. Tuck lemon slices inside each fish, along with a couple of rosemary sprigs and a few garlic slices. Scatter the onion over the fish and pour 2 tablespoons of cider or apple juice over each fish.

3 Wrap the foil loosely around each fish to make a parcel and bake for 25 minutes. Serve with boiled potatoes sprinkled with parsley.

• Per serving: 460 calories, protein 37g, carbohydrate 7g, fat 31g, saturated fat 6g, fiber 1g, added sugar none, salt 0.32g

An easy supper for a crowd,
this dish is cooked and served in one pan.

Shrimp and Tomato Pasta Bake

1lb leeks, thinly sliced
2lb ripe tomatoes, quartered
3 tbsp olive oil
salt & pepper to taste
1lb 5oz tubular pasta,
such as penne or rigatoni
8oz peeled and cleaned shrimp,
thawed if frozen
2 tbsp sundried tomato paste
½ cup vegetable stock
3 tbsp roughly chopped
fresh parsley
4oz heavy cream cream
5oz fresh mozzarella,
grated or finely chopped
4 tbsp freshly grated
parmesan cheese
1 thick slice of bread,
made into crumbs

Takes 1¼ hours • Serves 8

1 Preheat the oven to 400°F. Put the leeks and tomatoes in a large roasting pan and drizzle on the olive oil. Season and mix well. Roast for 30 minutes.
2 Meanwhile, cook the pasta for about 10–12 minutes until tender, then drain. Add to the roasting pan along with the shrimp. Season with salt and pepper. Mix the tomato paste into the stock and stir into the pasta. Sprinkle with parsley, then drizzle with cream. Scatter mozzarella, parmesan and breadcrumbs over the top.
3 Return to the oven for 15–20 minutes, until the topping is crisp and golden. Serve straight from the pan.

• Per serving: 506 calories, protein 21g, carbohydrate 65g, fat 20g, saturated fat 9g, fiber 5g, added sugar none, salt 0.65g

Skinless chicken breasts get a colorful
coating and a flavor boost.

Chicken with a Red Pepper Crust

4 boneless, skinless chicken breasts
salt & pepper to taste
1 small red pepper, roughly chopped
2 garlic cloves, finely chopped
large handful of fresh parsley
2 tbsp olive oil
pasta or new potatoes, and
green salad, to serve

Takes 30 minutes • Serves 4

1 Preheat the oven to 400°F. Put the chicken
breasts in a roasting tin or shallow ovenproof dish.
Season with salt and pepper.
2 Put the red pepper and garlic in a food processor
with the parsley and pulse a few times until coarsely
chopped. Stir in the oil and season generously.
Spread the crust over the chicken.
3 Spoon 2 tablespoons of water into the bottom of
the dish and roast the chicken, uncovered, for 25
minutes. Serve with pasta or new potatoes and a
green salad.

• Per serving: 210 calories, protein 23g, carbohydrate 5g, fat
11g, saturated fat 2g, fiber 1g, added sugar none, salt 0.19g

Couscous is the perfect partner for this dish, and will only need to be soaked and then fluffed up with a fork.

Moroccan Chicken

4 boneless, skinless chicken thighs,
1lb 2oz in total
1 cup chicken or vegetable stock
2 onions, finely chopped
3 tbsp olive oil
1 tbsp honey
1 tsp ground cumin
1 tsp ground coriander
good pinch chili powder
good pinch ground cinnamon
salt & pepper to taste
8oz zucchini, cut into sticks
15oz can chickpeas, drained
3 tbsp chopped fresh parsley
juice of 1 lemon
couscous or cooked rice, to serve

Takes 50 minutes • Serves 4

1 Put the chicken, stock, onions, oil, honey, herbs and spices in a pan, and season with salt and pepper. Bring to a boil, cover and cook gently for 25 minutes until the chicken is tender.

2 Add the zucchini and chickpeas and cook for 10 minutes.

3 Stir in the parsley and the lemon juice. Season to taste. Serve with couscous or rice.

• Per serving: 539 calories, protein 39g, carbohydrate 52g, fat 21g, saturated fat 4g, fiber 6g, added sugar 3g, salt 1.12g

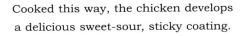

Cooked this way, the chicken develops
a delicious sweet-sour, sticky coating.

Lemon and Honey Chicken

3 lemons
2oz butter
3 tbsp honey
1 garlic clove, finely chopped
4 rosemary sprigs, leaves stripped
from the stalks
salt & pepper to taste
8 chicken pieces, such as
thighs and drumsticks
1lb 10oz potatoes, cut into
smallish chunks
green salad, to serve

Takes 1 hour 20 minutes • Serves 4

1 Preheat the oven to 400°F. Squeeze the juice
from 2 lemons and put in a small pan with the butter, honey, garlic and rosemary, and season with salt
and pepper. Heat gently until the butter melts.
2 Arrange the chicken in one layer in a
shallow roasting pan. Place the potatoes around the
chicken. Drizzle the lemon-herb butter over the
chicken and potatoes, turning the potatoes until they
are evenly coated. Cut the remaining lemon into 8
wedges and nestle among the potatoes.
3 Roast the chicken for 50 minutes to 1 hour,
mixing a few times, until the chicken is cooked and
the potatoes are crisp and golden. Serve with a
green salad.

• Per serving: 647 calories, protein 39g, carbohydrate 47g, fat
35g, saturated fat 14g, fiber 3g, added sugar 12g, salt 0.06g

...he vegetables; add green beans or
...nstead of asparagus and sugar snap peas.

...en with Spring Vegetables

2 tbsp olive oil
1 onion, finely chopped
4 boneless, skinless chicken thighs,
each cut in half
1lb 9oz new potatoes,
halved if large
8oz carrots, sliced
1 bay leaf
1 cup chicken stock
salt & pepper to taste
6 oz sugar snap peas
9oz asparagus, cut in 2-inch pieces
juice of 1 lemon
handful of fresh tarragon, chopped
6oz crème fraîche (or heavy cream
mixed with 1/2 tsp buttermilk)

1 Heat the oil in a large pan, add the onion and
chicken and cook for 5 minutes until the chicken
starts to brown. Add the potatoes, carrots and bay
leaf and saute 3 minutes, stirring to prevent the
chicken from sticking. Pour in the stock and then
season with salt and pepper.
2 Bring to the boil, then cover and simmer for 20
minutes, until the potatoes and chicken are cooked.
Add the sugar snap peas and asparagus and cook 3
minutes more.
3 Remove the bay leaf and stir in the lemon juice,
tarragon and crème fraîche. Check the seasoning
and serve.

• Per serving: 511 calories, protein 32g, carbohydrate 41g, fat
25g, saturated fat 10g, fiber 5g, added sugar none, salt 0.71g

Takes 40 minutes • Serves 4

A substantial meal all by itself—
no accompaniments needed.

Chicken and Red Pepper Pie

2 tbsp vegetable oil
1 small onion, chopped
3 boneless, skinless chicken
breasts, cut into chunks
1 red pepper, seeded and sliced
6oz broccoli, cut into small
florets (including stems), chopped
salt & pepper to taste
15oz package puff pastry
(2 sheets), thawed
5oz ready-made cheese
and chive dip
milk or beaten egg, to glaze

Takes 1 hour • Serves 4

1 Heat the oil in a frying pan and saute the onion for about 3 minutes, until it starts to brown. Add the chicken and cook, stirring, for 5 minutes. Add the pepper and broccoli and saute for 8–10 minutes, until everything is just cooked. Season. Cool slightly. Preheat the oven to 400°F.

2 Spread out a pasty sheet and place it on a dampened baking sheet. Spoon over the chicken mixture, leaving a 1-inch border all the way around. Dot spoonfuls of cheese and chive dip all over. Brush the pastry edges with water, top with the other pastry sheet and fold the edges of the bottom sheet over the top one, pressing to seal. Lightly score the surface.

3 Brush the pastry with milk or beaten egg and bake for 25–30 minutes, until the pastry is puffed and golden.

• Per serving: 727 calories, protein 35g, carbohydrate 46g, fat 46g, saturated fat 1g, fiber 2g, added sugar none, salt 1.33g

Make a breast of chicken go farther
with canned chickpeas and frozen vegetables.

Chicken and Chickpea Chili

1 tbsp olive oil
1 large onion, roughly chopped
1 boneless skinless chicken
breast, sliced
2 garlic cloves, finely chopped
1 tbsp chili powder
1 tsp ground cumin
15oz can chopped tomatoes
16fl oz vegetable stock
1 tsp sugar
15oz can chickpeas, drained
10oz frozen vegetables (carrots,
cauliflower, broccoli, etc.)
salt & pepper to taste

TO SERVE
5 oz sour cream
2oz grated cheddar cheese
generous handful of tortilla chips

Takes 50 minutes • Serves 4

1 Heat the oil in a large saucepan and saute the onion for 5–6 minutes until golden. Add the chicken and cook until golden brown. Add the garlic and spices and cook for 1 minute.

2 Stir in the tomatoes, stock and sugar. Bring to a boil, cover and simmer 25 minutes. Add the chickpeas and frozen vegetables, bring back to a boil, then simmer for 10 minutes.

3 Season with salt and pepper. Serve with a spoonful of sour cream, a sprinkling of cheddar and some tortilla chips on the side.

• Per serving: 374 calories, protein 22.8g, carbohydrate 28.3g, fat 19.6g, saturated fat 7.9g, fiber 6.3g, added sugar 1.3g, salt 1.51g

Frozen potato wedges and chops are cooked
together in one pan in the oven.

Lamb Chop and Potato Bake

3 tbsp olive oil
2 large onions, peeled and sliced
26oz frozen hot and spicy
potato wedges
8 small lamb chops
1 tsp dried thyme
½ cup lamb or chicken stock
1 tbsp tomato paste
salt & pepper to taste

Takes 40 minutes • Serves 4

1 Preheat the oven to 425°F. Heat a large roasting pan on the stove top, then add 2 tablespoons of the olive oil.

2 Put the onions in the roasting pan and saute for about 5 minutes, stirring often, until golden. Remove from the heat. Scatter the potato wedges. Put the chops on top, sprinkle with thyme and drizzle with the remaining oil.

3 Bake for 20 minutes. Mix the stock with the tomato paste and pour around the chops in the pan. Bake for 10 minutes until everything is brown and crisp. Season with salt and pepper, and serve.

• Per serving: 680 calories, protein 33g, carbohydrate 39g, fat 45g, saturated fat 19g, fiber 4g, added sugar none, salt 0.43g

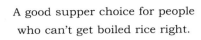

A good supper choice for people who can't get boiled rice right.

One-pot Lamb with Rice

2 tbsp olive oil
1½ lb boneless lamb (leg or shoulder), cut into1in cubes
2 onions, roughly chopped
2 tsp ground cumin
2 tsp ground coriander
6oz long grain rice
2 tsp dried oregano
3 tbsp tomato paste
grated zest and juice of 1 lemon
salt & pepper to taste
2 tbsp chopped fresh parsley

Takes 55 minutes • Serves 4

1 Heat the oil in a large frying pan with a cover. Add the lamb and cook over high heat, stirring constantly, for 5 minutes, until browned on all sides. Add the onions and cook 2–3 minutes more, until softened. Add the cumin and coriander and saute for another minute.

2 Stir in the rice and oregano. Mix the tomato paste, lemon zest and juice with 3 cups boiling water and pour into the pan. Stir well and season with salt and pepper.

3 Bring to a boil, then simmer for 20–25 minutes until the lamb and rice are cooked. Stir in the parsley and serve right from the pan.

• Per serving: 563 calories, protein 36g, carbohydrate 47g, fat 27g, saturated fat 11g, fiber 1g, added sugar none, salt 0.34g

Dates and cranberry sauce add sweetness
and succulence to the lamb.

Lamb and Date Casserole

1lb 4oz boneless lamb, diced
1 tbsp all-purpose flour
2 tbsp olive oil
2 onions, chopped
3 large carrots, cut into chunks
2 garlic cloves, finely chopped
2 cups chicken, lamb or
vegetable stock
1 tbsp cranberry sauce
2 tsp tomato paste
12 pitted dates
3 tbsp chopped fresh parsley
rice or steamed couscous, to serve

Takes 1 hour • Serves 4

1 Put the lamb and flour in a plastic bag and shake well, until coated. Heat the olive oil in a large frying pan. Remove the lamb from the bag and shake off any excess flour, then add to the pan with the onions and carrots. Cook over medium to high heat for 8–10 minutes, stirring often, until golden.
2 Stir in the garlic and cook for 1 minute. Pour in the stock and bring to a boil. Reduce the heat and simmer, covered, for 20 minutes, until slightly thickened.
3 Stir in the cranberry sauce, tomato paste salt & pepper to taste, dates and parsley. Season with salt and pepper. Serve with rice or steamed couscous.

• Per serving: 466 calories, protein 32g, carbohydrate 48g, fat 18g, saturated fat 6g, fiber 5g, added sugar 1g, salt 0.81g

You can make up the savory bean mix
the day before you cook the chops.

Lamb and Bean Hotpot

2 onions, chopped
3 tbsp olive oil
2 garlic cloves, chopped
2 × 15oz can cannellini, great
northern, navy or any white beans
1 tsp dried oregano
½ cup vegetable stock
6oz can chopped tomatoes
salt & pepper to taste
8 lamb chops or pork chops

Takes 55 minutes • Serves 4

1 Preheat the oven to 400°F. Saute the onions in 2 tablespoons of the oil for 5 minutes. Add the garlic, beans and half the oregano and stir briefly. Add the stock and tomatoes, season with salt and pepper, and bring to a boil.

2 Put the bean mixture into an ovenproof dish big enough to hold the chops in a single layer. Lay the chops on top of the beans.

3 Sprinkle with the remaining oregano, drizzle with the remaining oil and season.Bake for 30 minutes until the chops are tender and nicely browned.

• Per serving: 518 calories, protein 39g, carbohydrate 30g, fat 28g, saturated fat 10g, fiber 9g, added sugar none, salt 1.67g

A lighter version of a popular dish, using pork instead
of beef and green beans instead of red kidney beans.

Summer Chili

2 tbsp oil
1 onion, chopped
1lb ground pork
2 garlic cloves, crushed
2 tsp mild chili powder
15oz can chopped tomatoes
2 tbsp tomato paste
2 cups chicken stock
1 red pepper, seeded and
cut into chunks
12oz new potatoes,
cut into chunks
9oz green beans, trimmed
warm crusty bread, to serve

Takes 50 minutes • Serves 4

1 Heat the oil in a large frying pan and saute the
onion and ground pork for 3–4 minutes, stirring
occasionally.
2 Add the garlic, chili powder, tomatoes, tomato
paste, chicken stock, red pepper and new potatoes.
Bring to a boil, cover and simmer over low heat for
15 minutes until the potatoes are just tender.
3 Stir in the green beans, re-cover the pan and
continue to cook for 5 minutes, until the beans are
tender but crisp. Serve with warm crusty bread.

• Per serving: 390 calories, protein 30g, carbohydrate 26g, fat
19g, saturated fat 5g, fiber 4g, added sugar none, salt 0.94g

pork is economical when feeding a crowd.
Sliced potatoes make it filling.

ork and Potato Hotpot

1 tbsp olive oil
1 onion, chopped
2 garlic cloves, crushed
2lb 4oz ground pork or beef
1 tbsp all-purpose flour
1½ cups chicken or vegetable stock
1 tsp dried rosemary or thyme
2 tbsp Worcestershire sauce
4 tbsp tomato paste
3lb 5oz potatoes, peeled
1oz butter
steamed green vegetables, to serve

Takes 2 hours • Serves 8

1 Preheat the oven to 375°F. Heat the oil and saute the onion and garlic for 3–4 minutes. Add the meat and cook 5–6 minutes more.

2 Stir in the flour and cook for 1 minute. Add the stock, then stir in the rosemary or thyme, Worcestershire sauce and tomato paste. Bring to a boil, then simmer for 30 minutes. Meanwhile, cook the potatoes in boiling salted water for 10 minutes. Drain and slice thickly.

3 Spoon half the meat mixture into a 8 × 12 × 2, 3-inch deep ovenproof dish and cover with half the potatoes. Repeat the layers, dot the top with butter and bake for 1 hour. Serve with steamed green vegetables.

• Per serving: 407 calories, protein 29g, carbohydrate 38g, fat 17g, saturated fat 6g, fiber 3g, added sugar none, salt 0.64g

A really quick and easy meal –
the perfect (lazy!) TV dinner.

Sausage and Corn Hash

1 tbsp olive oil
14oz sausages (use your favorite)
1lb 9oz new potatoes,
cut into chunks
salt & pepper to taste
6oz can corn, drained
2 tbsp chopped fresh cilantro
(coriander) or parsley
8oz spicy tomato salsa, to serve

Takes 30 minutes • Serves 4

1 Heat the oil in a large frying pan. Cut the
sausages into bite-size chunks and saute in the oil
until just cooked, about 10 minutes. Meanwhile,
bring a large pot of salted water to a boil, add the
potatoes and cook for 8–10 minutes. Drain well.
2 Put the potatoes into the frying pan, season with
salt and pepper, and cook over medium heat until
they take on a bit of color. Stir in the corn and heat
through. Adjust the seasoning.
3 Sprinkle with cilantro or parsley. Divide between
serving dishes and drizzle some salsa over the hash.

• Per serving: 519 calories, protein 17g, carbohydrate 56g, fat
27g, saturated fat 9g, fiber 4g, added sugar 4g, salt 4.09g

A straightforward recipe using
affordable ingredients.

Mustardy Sausages with Apple

1 tbsp vegetable oil
8 plump herbed sausages,
about 1lb
1 medium onion, cut into wedges
2 macintosh or other eating apples
(peel on), cored and
each cut into 8 wedges
1 rounded tbsp currant jelly
1 cup chicken stock (made
from a cube is fine)
2 tbsp grainy mustard
rosemary sprigs

Takes 25 minutes • Serves 4

1 Heat the oil in a large frying pan, add the sausages and saute for 5 minutes, turning often. Nestle the onion wedges among the sausages and continue to cook until everything starts to turn really golden, stirring every now and then. Turn up the heat, toss in the apples and let them take on a bit of color too, stirring carefully so that they don't break.
2 Stir the currant jelly into the stock until it dissolves, then stir in the mustard. Pour this mixture into the frying pan so everything bubbles fiercely for a few minutes to make a syrupy gravy.
3 Lower the heat, throw in the rosemary and simmer, uncovered, for 10 minutes until the sausages are cooked.

• Per serving: 368 calories, protein 16.7g, carbohydrate 21g, fat 24.7g, saturated fat 8.1g, fiber 2g, added sugar 3.2g, salt 2.68g

Wholegrain mustard adds
a kick to a favorite family supper.

Mustardy Toad

8 plump herbed sausages
2 onions, thinly sliced
1 tbsp vegetable oil
4oz all-purpose flour
salt & pepper to taste
2 eggs
½ cup milk mixed with ½ cup water
2 tbsp wholegrain mustard
cabbage or broccoli,
and gravy to serve

Takes 1 hour • Serves 4

1 Preheat the oven to 425°F. Put the sausages and onions in a roasting pan and drizzle with the oil. Roast for 15–20 minutes until the sausages just start to brown.
2 Sift the flour and a pinch of salt and pepper into a bowl. Make a well in the center, drop in the eggs and beat together. Gradually beat in the milk and water mixture, then stir in the the mustard.
3 Remove the roasting pan from the oven. Quickly pour in the batter and return to the oven for 35–40 minutes more, until the batter is risen and golden. Serve with cabbage or broccoli and gravy.

• Per serving: 562 calories, protein 24g, carbohydrate 37g, fat 36g, saturated fat 12g, fiber 3g, added sugar none, salt 2.72g

Although cobblers are more familiar as desserts,
they can make great savory dishes too.

Bacon and Tomato Cobbler

12 slices bacon
1 large onion, chopped
1 tbsp olive oil
4 stalks celery, thickly sliced
12oz crushed tomatoes
½ cup chicken stock
15oz can lima beans, drained
salt & pepper to taste

FOR THE COBBLER TOPPING
3oz butter, cut into pieces
8oz self-rising flour
2 tsp dried mixed herbs
salt
6fl oz milk

Takes 1¼ hours • Serves 4

1 Preheat the oven to 400°F. Cut 3 strips of bacon into small pieces and set aside. Cut the rest into 3 pieces per slice. Saute the onion in the oil for 2–3 minutes, add the large bacon pieces for 5–6 minutes and the celery for 3–4 minutes.

2 Add the tomatoes and stock, bring to a boil, cover and simmer for 20 minutes. Add the beans, then season with salt and pepper.

3 To make the cobbler topping, rub the butter into the flour. Stir in the herbs, a pinch of salt and the milk. Put the bean mixture into a large ovenproof dish. Spoon the topping over the beans and scatter the reserved bacon on top. Bake for 25–30 minutes until golden.

• Per serving: 855 calories, protein 31g, carbohydrate 63g, fat 58g, saturated fat 26g, fiber 6g, added sugar none, salt 4.74g

Ham and vegetables cooked in a mustardy sauce
and topped with pie crust—great for a crowd.

Chunky Ham Pie

1 tbsp olive oil
1 onion, chopped
1 garlic clove, crushed
1lb parsnips, roughly chopped
3 carrots, roughly chopped
2 celery stalks, thickly sliced
2 tbsp all-purpose flour
1lb cooked ham, cut into chunks
5oz heavy cream
1½ cups vegetable stock
2 tbsp wholegrain mustard
salt & pepper to taste
9 oz ready-made pie crust
1 tbsp milk
vegetables, to serve

Takes 1¼ hours • Serves 8

1 Preheat the oven to 375°F. Heat the oil in a large pan and saute the onion and garlic for 3–4 minutes. Stir in the parsnips and carrots and cook for 4–5 minutes, stirring frequently. Add the celery, sprinkle in the flour and cook for 1 minute, mixing thoroughly.

2 Add the ham and pour in the cream and stock. Stir in the mustard. Season with salt and pepper. Simmer for 5 minutes until slightly thickened, then spoon into a2-quart baking dish. Allow to cool slightly.

3 Use the pie crust to cover the pie, cutting off any excess. Brush with milk. Cut out leaf shapes from the pastry trimmings and put on top of the pie. Brush with milk again and bake for 30 minutes, until the crust is golden. Serve with vegetables.

• Per serving: 452 calories, protein 17g, carbohydrate 37g, fat 27g, saturated fat 12g, fiber 5g, added sugar none, salt 2.09g

A risotto cooked as a cake and served in
slices, with a good, ready-made tomato sauce.

Pesto Rice Cake

1oz butter
1 large leek (6oz), finely chopped
12oz arborio rice
3½ cups vegetable stock
4oz green pesto
2 eggs, beaten
black pepper to taste
5oz mozzarella, thinly sliced
your favorite jar of tomato sauce,
to serve

Takes 1 hour • Serves 4

1 Melt the butter in a frying pan and saute the leek
for 5–6 minutes, until soft. Stir in the rice. Pour in a
ladleful of stock and simmer until almost all the
stock has been absorbed. Continue to add stock
gradually and simmer, stirring continuously, for 20
minutes or until the rice is creamy.
2 Stir in the pesto, eggs and some black pepper.
Spoon half the rice mixture into a 9-inch non-stick
frying pan. Arrange the mozzarella slices on top and
spoon over the remaining rice. Cook over medium
heat for 4 minutes.
3 Put a plate over the frying pan and carefully invert
the rice cake, then slide it back into the pan to cook
the other side. Press to reshape it and cook for 4
minutes, until golden. Gently heat tomato sauce and
pour over rice.

• Per serving: 482 calories, protein 19g, carbohydrate 57g, fat
22g, saturated fat 9g, fiber 2g, added sugar none, salt 1.46g

Just three ingredients, but a luxurious finale to a meal. You can find lemon curd in many supermarkets, with the jams and jellies.

Lemon Curd Brûlée

16oz heavy cream
8oz good lemon curd
4–5 tsp confectioner's sugar

Takes 15 minutes, plus chilling • Serves 4

1 In a large bowl, whisk the cream with an electric beater until it just holds its shape. Stir in the lemon curd.
2 Spoon into six 3½-inch ramekins and smooth the tops. Chill for at least 1 hour, or overnight.
3 Preheat the broiler. Sift a thin layer of confectioner's sugar over each ramekin. broil about 2–3 minutes until the sugar has caramelized. Alternatively, you can use a kitchen blow torch to caramelize the sugar. Serve immediately.

• Per serving: 507 calories, protein 2g, carbohydrate 12g, fat 50g, saturated fat 32g, fiber none, added sugar 9g, salt 0.09g

It sounds rich, but this dessert is surprisingly light.
Make it up to four hours ahead of serving time.

Coffee Ricotta Creams

4 tbsp raisins
3 tbsp rum or brandy
6 tbsp strong black coffee
2oz sugar
8oz ricotta cheese
5oz heavy cream
2oz dark chocolate, grated
confectioner's sugar, for dusting

Takes 25 minutes, plus chilling • Serves 4

1 Mix together the raisins, rum or brandy, coffee and sugar. Stir well and set aside for at least 1 hour.
2 Put the ricotta in a bowl and beat lightly to soften. Gradually beat in the raisins, rum, coffee and sugar mixture. Whip the cream into soft peaks and fold into the ricotta with half the chocolate.
3 Spoon into four glasses and sprinkle on the remaining chocolate. Chill until you are ready to serve. Dust lightly with confectioner's sugar before serving.

• Per serving: 447 calories, protein 8g, carbohydrate 39g, fat 28g, saturated fat 17g, fiber 1g, added sugar 22g, salt 0.23g

With an original flavor for an ice cream,
this dessert has an unusual but elegant taste.

Iced Ginger Cream

6 ready-made individual meringues
16oz heavy cream
grated zest of 1 lemon
3 tbsp kirsch (cherry liqueur)
2 tbsp fine sugar
4 pieces of crystallized ginger in
syrup, finely chopped

Takes 20 minutes, plus chilling • Serves 6

1 Line a 7-inch round cake pan with plastic wrap.
Break the meringues into chunks. Whip the cream
until just stiff, then fold in the lemon zest, kirsch,
sugar, ginger and meringue pieces.
2 Spoon into the pan, level the top and put in the
freezer for at least 4 hours.
3 Turn out of the pan 10 minutes before serving
and chill. Cut into wedges and drizzle with the syrup
from the jar of ginger.

• Per serving: 333 calories, protein 2g, carbohydrate 22g, fat
26g, saturated fat 16g, none, added sugar 19g, salt 0.54g

Tart fruits, cooked in butter and sugar,
make a tempting sauce for ice cream.

Apple Blackberry Ice Cream Sauce

3oz butter
3oz fine, light brown sugar
4 apples, such as macintosh,
peeled, cored and cut into
wedges
4oz blackberries
juice of 1 lemon
vanilla ice cream, to serve

Takes 20 minutes • Serves 4

1 Heat the butter and sugar in a frying pan. When the butter has melted and the sugar has dissolved, stir in the apples.

2 Cook for 5–7 minutes, stirring occasionally, until the apples are tender and the sauce is beginning to caramelize and brown. Immediately remove the pan from the heat and add the blackberries.

3 Stir in the lemon juice and serve spooned over scoops of vanilla ice cream.

• Per serving: 302 calories, protein 1g, carbohydrate 37g, fat 18g, saturated fat 11g, fiber 3g, added sugar 22g, salt 0.42g

Raid the fruit bowl and the pantry
to make a tempting pudding.

Banana Sesame Fritters

4oz self-rising flour
2 tbsp toasted sesame seeds
1 tbsp fine sugar,
plus extra for sprinkling
4 bananas, peeled
vegetable oil, for deep frying
maple syrup, to serve

Takes 30 minutes • Serves 4

1 Mix the flour, sesame seeds and sugar in a bowl. Make a well in the center and beat in ½ cup cold water to make a smooth batter.
2 Cut each banana into four diagonal slices. Fill a large pan or wok a third full with oil and heat until hot. Dip the bananas in the batter, then carefully lower them into the oil with a slotted spoon.
3 Fry for 3–4 minutes, until crisp. Drain on paper towels. Serve hot, sprinkled with sugar and drizzled with maple syrup.

• Per serving: 345 calories, protein 5g, carbohydrate 51g, fat 15g, saturated fat 2g, fiber 3g, added sugar 7g, salt 0.26g

Look for ready-made pancakes, refrigerated or frozen, in the super-market. Or you can use the leftovers from breakfast.

Pancake Streudels

3oz butter
3oz light brown sugar
6 eating apples, such as macintosh,
peeled, cored, and
each cut into 12 wedges
3oz pecans, roughly chopped
3oz raisins
squeeze of lemon juice
6 ready-made pancakes
confectioner's sugar, to dust

Takes 25 minutes • Serves 6

1 Heat the butter and sugar in a frying pan, stirring until dissolved. Toss in the apples and cook, stirring gently, for 3–4 minutes until softened. Add the nuts and let them brown a little.

2 Remove from the heat and stir in the raisins and lemon juice. Spoon some filling into the center of each pancake.

3 Fold two sides of the pancake into the center to overlap over the filling slightly. Bring the third side over, then flip the whole pancake over to make a square pouch. Cut in half diagonally and serve with a generous sprinkling of confectioner's sugar.

• Per serving: 478 calories, protein 6g, carbohydrate 55g, fat 27g, saturated fat 9g, fiber 4g, added sugar 16g, salt 0.41g

Save time with pre-cut pineapple,
or the canned fruit sold in natural juice.

Baked Pineapple Pudding

1 large pineapple, peeled,
cored and chopped
3oz light brown sugar
3 tbsp all-purpose flour
finely grated zest of 1 orange

FOR THE TOPPING
5oz all-purpose flour
2oz ground almonds, toasted
3oz finer sugar
2½ tsp baking powder
¼ tsp salt
1 egg, beaten
5 tbsp plain yogurt
3oz butter, melted and cooled
½ tsp vanilla extract
2 tbsp toasted almond slivers

Takes 1 hour 20 minutes • Serves 6

1 Preheat the oven to 375°F. Butter a large baking dish. Put the pineapple, sugar, flour and orange zest in a bowl and toss well. Spread out in the baking dish.
2 Mix together the flour, ground almonds, sugar, baking powder and salt. Add the egg, yogurt, butter and vanilla, and stir to combine. Drop spoonfuls over the fruit, leaving a 1-inch border.
3 Sprinkle with slivered almonds. Bake for 50–55 minutes, until a skewer inserted in the center comes out clean. Serve warm.

• Per serving: 492 calories, protein 8g, carbohydrate 72g, fat 21g, saturated fat 8g, fiber 4g, added sugar 29g, salt 1.19g

A rich and fruity version of bread and
butter pudding using up buns or fruit breads.

Hot Cross Bun Pudding

2oz butter
6 hot cross buns, split in half
(fresh or slightly stale)
1 cup milk
1 cup cream
1 tsp vanilla extract
1 tsp ground cinnamon
4oz light brown sugar
4 eggs
2 tbsp fine sugar, for sprinkling

Takes 50 minutes • Serves 6

1 Preheat the oven to 350°F. Butter a 9-inch
ovenproof dish, 2 inches deep. Butter the buns and
lay them in the dish, buttered side up, so they slightly overlap. Pour the milk and cream into another pan
and add the vanilla essence and half the cinnamon.
Heat gently until it just comes to a boil, then remove
from the heat.
2 In a bowl, whisk together the sugar and eggs until
frothy, then whisk in the warm milk mixture. Pour
evenly over the buns. Let stand for 5 minutes.
3 Sprinkle the remaining cinnamon over the buns
and bake for 30 minutes, until set. Sprinkle with fine
sugar while still warm.

• Per serving: 484 calories, protein 11g, carbohydrate 57g, fat
25g, saturated fat 14g, fiber 1g, added sugar 30g, salt 0.58g

You can substitute other fruits or fruit mixtures—
berries and peaches make nice alternatives.

Blueberry and Apple Cobbler

1 cooking apple, such as Granny
Smith, about 6oz
9oz blueberries
2oz light brown sugar
8 oz mascarpone cheese

FOR THE COBBLER TOPPING
3oz butter, cut into pieces
8oz self-rising flour
2oz light brown sugar
grated zest of 1 lemon
5oz plain yogurt

Takes 40 minutes • Serves 6

1 Preheat the oven to 425°F. Peel, core and thinly slice the apple and put into a 2-quart ovenproof dish. Scatter over the blueberries on top, sprinkle with the sugar and gently stir. Spoon the mascarpone cheese on top.

2 To make the topping, rub the butter into the flour or process in a food processor until it looks like fine breadcrumbs. Stir in the sugar and lemon zest. Make a well in the center and add the yogurt. Stir until evenly combined, but do not overmix.

3 Spoon the cobbler mixture onto the fruit and mascarpone. Bake for 20 minutes, until the topping is risen and golden and the filling is bubbling.

• Per serving: 323 calories, protein 5g, carbohydrate 49g, fat 13g, saturated fat 8g, fiber 2g, added sugar 17g, salt 0.66g

Don't be put off by the cooking time; you only
need to add water once or twice while the pudding cooks.

Steamed Rhubarb Pudding

12oz rhubarb, cut into chunks
3oz sugar
1 tsp ground ginger
4½oz unsalted butter,
plus extra for greasing
4½oz fine sugar
few drops vanilla extract
2 medium eggs
6oz self-rising flour
cream or custard, to serve

Takes 1 hour 50 minutes • Serves 6

1 Cook the rhubarb, sugar and ginger over a low heat for 3 minutes. Grease a 1-quart heatproof bowl and add the rhubarb.
2 Cream the butter and fine sugar together until fluffy. Add the vanilla extract. Beat in the eggs one at a time, then mix in the flour. Spoon the mixture smoothly onto the rhubarb. Make a pleat across the center of a piece of buttered waxed paper. Place over the bowl, butter-side down, cover with foil and tie with string.
3 Place the bowl in a large pot and add enough boiling water to half fill the pot. Bring to a boil. Cover and simmer for 1½ hours, occasionally adding boiling water as necessary. Lift out the bowl, remove the coverings and turn the pudding out onto a plate. Serve with cream or custard.

• Per serving: 416 calories, protein 6g, carbohydrate 58g, fat 20g, saturated fat 11g, fiber 2g, added sugar 35g, salt 0.34g

A new spin on good old-fashioned
pecan pie.

Pecan Tart

1oz self-rising flour
5oz all-purpose flour
3oz cold butter, cut into pieces
heavy cream, to serve

FOR THE FILLING
3oz butter, at room temperature
5oz light brown sugar
2 eggs, well beaten
4oz golden syrup
2 tbsp heavy cream
4oz pecans, roughly chopped

Takes 1 hour 10 minutes • Serves 8

1 Preheat the oven to 375°F. Rub both the flours and butter into fine crumbs. Add 2–3 tablespoons cold water and stir with a pastry knife until a dough forms.

2 Shape into a ball, roll out and line a shallow 9-inch fluted tart pan. Line with parchment paper and a handful of dried beans, and bake for 17 minutes. Remove the beans and paper and cook 5 minutes more.

3 To make the filling, beat the butter and sugar until pale and fluffy, then gradually beat in the eggs, syrup and cream. Mix in the nuts. Transfer to the tart pan and bake for 30–35 minutes, until set. Cool in the pan, remove and serve with cream.

• Per serving: 456 calories, protein 5g, carbohydrate 45g, fat 30g, saturated fat 13g, fiber 1g, added sugar 28g, salt 0.58g

Put the cookies in a plastic bag and
crush them with a rolling pin.

Chocolate and Ginger Nut Slices

4oz unsalted butter,
plus extra for greasing
7oz plain (unsweetened) chocolate
2 tbsp golden syrup
8oz ginger snaps, crushed
4oz hazelnuts, toasted and chopped

Takes 20 minutes, plus chilling • Serves 8

1 Lightly grease a 7-inch round pan. In a heatproof bowl set over a pan of simmering water, heat the butter, 4oz chocolate and the syrup, stirring occasionally, until melted.

2 Remove from the heat and stir in the cookie crumbs and three-quarters of the nuts. Press the mixture into the pan.

3 Melt the remaining chocolate, spoon on top of the mixture and sprinkle on the remaining nuts. Chill for 1 hour before serving, cut into slices.

• Per serving: 433 calories, protein 4g, carbohydrate 39g, fat 30g, saturated fat 13g, fiber 2g, added sugar 20g, salt 0.68g

Lightly crush the oats for a chewy result,
or use rolled oats for a crunchy finish.

Classic Oat Flapjacks

6oz butter, cut into pieces
5oz golden syrup
2oz light brown sugar
9oz whole oats

Takes 35 minutes • Serves 12

1 Preheat the oven to 350°F. Line the base of a shallow 9-inch square pan with a sheet of baking parchment.

2 Put the butter, syrup and sugar in a medium saucepan. Stir over a low heat until the butter has melted and the sugar has dissolved. Remove from the heat and stir in the oats.

3 Press the mixture into the baking pan. Bake for 20–25 minutes, until golden brown on top. Let cool in the pan for 5 minutes, then score into bars or squares with the back of a knife while still warm. Cool in the pan completely before cutting and removing—this prevents the flapjack from breaking.

• Per serving: 242 calories, protein 3g, carbohydrate 29g, fat 14g, saturated fat 8g, fiber 1g, added sugar 13g, salt 0.38g

Picture credits and recipe credits

BBC Worldwide would like to thank the following for providing photographs. While every effort has been made to trace and acknowledge all photographers, we would like to apologise should there be any errors or omissions.

Chris Alack p71, p79, p91, p93; Marie-Louise Avery p53, p117; Jean Cazals p155, p187, p189; Ken Field p87, p115, p125; Dave King p75, p173, p183; William Lingwood p197; David Munns p41, p45, p49, p69, p105, p129, p135, p145, p147, p191, p199, p209; William Reavell p19, p157; Howard Shooter p57; Simon Smith p37, p111; Roger Stowell p15, p17, p21, p25, p27, p31, p33, p35, p39, p43, p51, p59, p61, p63, p65, p67, p77, p81, p85, p87, p95, p97, p101, p103, p113, p119, p123, p127, p131, p133, p137, p139, p149, p151, p159, p163, p165, p167, p169, p175, p177, p179, p181, p193, p195, p201; Sam Stowell p141, p143; Martin Thompson p11, p13, p23, p29, p47, p55, p83, p121, p161, p171; Martin Thompson and Philip Webb p73, p99; Ian Wallace p207; Philip Webb p211; Simon Wheeler p89, p107; Jonathan Whitaker p203; BBC Worldwide p153, p185, p205

All the recipes in this book have been created by the editorial teams on *BBC Good Food Magazine* and *BBC Vegetarian Good Food Magazine*.

Angela Boggiano, Lorna Brash, Sara Buenfeld, Mary Cadogan, Gilly Cubitt, Barney Desmazery, Joanna Farrow, Rebecca Ford, Silvana Franco, Catherine Hill, Jane Lawrie, Clare Lewis, Sara Lewis, Liz Martin, Kate Moseley, Orlando Murrin, Vicky Musselman, Angela Nilsen, Justine Pattison, Jenny White and Jeni Wright.

Index